MODERN CHRISTIAN REVOLUTIONARIES SERIES

General Editor:
DONALD ATTWATER

DICK SHEPPARD: MAN OF PEACE

He who praises a man ought to follow him, and if he be not ready to follow him he ought not to praise him.—*St. John Chrysostom.*

MODERN CHRISTIAN REVOLUTIONARIES

DICK SHEPPARD: MAN OF PEACE

By
CHARLES H. S. MATTHEWS, M.A.,
CANON EMERITUS OF COVENTRY

Author of *A Parson in the Australian Bush,
The Roots of Religion,* etc.

WIPF & STOCK · Eugene, Oregon

TO
PETER AND PAM

Wipf and Stock Publishers
199 W 8th Ave, Suite 3
Eugene, OR 97401

Dick Sheppard
Man of Peace
By Matthews, Charles H. S.
Copyright©1948 James Clarke Lutterworth Press
ISBN 13: 978-1-5326-8695-5
Publication date 4/2/2019
Previously published by James Clarke & Co. LTD., 1948

PREFACE

IT has been no easy matter to write this book. It has been written, under conditions most unconducive to literary work, at odd moments snatched from work of many other kinds. And all through its composition I have been conscious of the fact that most people who did not know Dick Sheppard personally, and, as I gladly admit, some of those who did know him, have accepted as authoritative the portrait of Dick painted—and from a purely literary point of view brilliantly painted—by Mr Ellis Roberts in his *H. R. L. Sheppard, Life and Letters*. And this has created another difficulty for me. The very different judgements passed on Mr Roberts's book by Dick's friends is in itself a warning to anyone else who attempts to write about that wholly lovable, but many-sided and elusive, being. I know one or two friends of Dick's who are almost enthusiastic in its praise, and others who, however much they may admire its qualities as a piece of literature, can hardly find words strong enough to condemn it as a portrait of their beloved friend and, in some instances, colleague.

But despite these difficulties, which I realized from the first, I wanted to write this book, as my personal tribute to one who for a long period of years was one of the dearest of my friends. The labour of writing it has been, in very truth, a labour of love. I have tried to let Dick speak largely for himself, and I am more than grateful to Mr John Murray and Messrs. Methuen & Co. for permission to publish long extracts from his books published by them. I am also deeply indebted to many friends, among them the Reverend Hugh Johnston, who was for so many years Dick's colleague at St Martin-in-the-Fields, Dr Maude

Royden-Shaw, Mrs Ewan Hay, Mr J. McClemens, and last but not least to Dick's own daughter, Mrs Richardson, for the way in which they have helped me to make my little book less inadequate than it would otherwise have been.

C. H. S. M.

BIBLIOGRAPHY

Some books by H. R. L. Sheppard:

Two Days Before. Simple thoughts about our Lord on the Cross (S.C.M. Press, 1924).

The Human Parson (John Murray, 1924).

The Impatience of a Parson (Hodder & Stoughton, 1927).

We Say "No": The Plain Man's Guide to Pacifism (John Murray, 1935).

My Cry for Christianity (Cassell, 1936).

If I Were Dictator (Methuen, 1935).

Books about H. R. L. Sheppard:

Dick Sheppard by his Friends (Hodder & Stoughton).

H. R. L. Sheppard: Life and Letters. By R. Ellis Roberts (Murray).

CONTENTS

Preface	5
Bibliography	7
I. All Things to All Men	11
II. Dick as I knew Him	15
III. At St Martin-in-the-Fields	36
IV. Was He a Revolutionary?	41
V. Editor, Journalist, Broadcaster	51
VI. "The Human Parson" and His Axiom	60
VII. Warring World and Divided Church	72

1

All Things to All Men

"I AM become all things to all men that I may by all means save some." That saying of St Paul may be said to sum up the whole ministry of Dick Sheppard. And that is precisely what makes it so difficult—nay, so impossible—for any one among his innumerable friends to write his life, or to attempt to give an account of his ministry, which will seem in the least adequate to hundreds of other friends, each one of whom knew and loved his own individual Dick Sheppard.

Mr Ellis Roberts has given us his own brilliant picture of Dick as he saw him; or rather, of the two individuals he seemed to discover—the shy tormented "Lawrie," in whom unwise and unkind treatment in his childhood had produced an abiding "inferiority complex"; and "Dick," the beloved idol of thousands, on whom as individuals, or as the multitude of "sheep, having no shepherd," he lavished his compassion, not in easy words of comfort but in that continual and unending self-giving, which indeed in the end cost him his very life.

Mr Roberts, probably because he never knew Dick personally until the very end of his life, when he was indeed a mortally sick man, never knew him, as so many of us remember him, in the days when he was really in his prime, seems to me and to many others among Dick's friends to give an unduly sombre picture of his life and an unduly simplified interpretation of Dick's complex character. Indeed, to many of us Mr Roberts seems to become the slave of his own ingenious theory and to paint a picture of a pathetic, psychopathic individual which does much less than justice to the Dick we knew and loved for so many years.

The truth is, as Miss Rose Macaulay says in an amusing passage in one of her books, that "we are all of us mixed and most of us not very well mixed," but it is just that "mixedness" which produces an inner tension out of which true character is fashioned. The present writer, who like Dick had a most unhappy childhood and suffered acutely from bullying at school, can sympathize profoundly with Dick's unhappiness at Marlborough, of which Mr Roberts makes so much, and yet feel that without that tragic experience Dick would never have achieved the profound sympathy with and understanding of suffering humanity which made him what he became. The "mixture" in Dick was, I am convinced, much less simple than Mr Roberts suggests. The Master of the Temple, a close friend of Dick's for many years, has written that in his opinion the real dichotomy in Dick was less between the "Lawrie" and the "Dick" of Mr Roberts's imagination than between "the descendant of Napoleon" (which Dick was, according to a family tradition) "and the profoundly humble servant of Christ."

The Dean of St Paul's, another great friend of Dick's, seems to me to get even nearer to the truth, when he says in a letter to the present writer, "Of course the general idea of there being several Dick Sheppards is true enough. I should have said there were four or five and not only two."

My own belief is that Mr Bernard Shaw's comment, when he heard of Dick's death, really goes very near the root of the matter: "All that they will say of him will be quite true. And what an actor! *What* an actor!" For the real genius among actors is surely the man who embraces in himself so many individuals that he not merely *plays*, but for the time being *is* the person whom he is acting. So, I believe, it was with Dick. He actually became "all things to all men" because he was in himself, to such an unusual degree, a kind of epitome of humanity.

But what made Dick, in spite of all his complexity, really one integral and unique person was the fact that, like St Paul, he was possessed by the unifying, purposeful passion of love, so that he became all things to all men that he might "by all means save some."

One other preliminary observation must, I think, be made to explain what might otherwise seem the entirely unaccountable variations which many of Dick's friends have noticed in the accounts he gave to different persons at different times of incidents in his life.

Dick had the kind of dramatic, visualizing imagination—not uncommon among those who have Celtic blood in their veins—which made him see again—and see very vividly—the past events on which his memory was focussed. As he saw these events his imagination was (as I believe, quite unconsciously) at work upon them, adding little details and dramatic touches which made the story as he told it so much more than a mere recital of dead facts. Dick was, as we all realized, among other things a born story-teller.[1]

This explains for me astonishing differences between stories as Dick told them to me, of various incidents in his life, and stories of the same incidents as they appear in Mr Roberts's book. This is notably true in regard to Dick's early experiences at Marlborough, to which I shall return

---

[1] Perhaps I may be allowed to illustrate this point from my own experience, for I too have the visualizing type of memory. Some forty years ago, immediately after my return from five years' work in the Australian Bush, I wrote an account of my life there. Since that time I have addressed innumerable audiences on life and work in the Bush and have retold many times stories first recorded in my book. But, on re-reading my own book after many years, I was astonished to find how much they had changed in the course of years, as imaginative memory had played upon them; and this has happened not consciously but quite unconsciously, just as I am convinced it happened in Dick's case.

later, and also in the account of the appointment of his successor at St Martin-in-the Fields.

But all this only goes to prove that every close friend of Dick saw his own unique Dick, the Dick who gave himself away so freely to that particular friend, as though he were the only friend he had in the world; and gave himself in just that particular way which that friend seemed to demand. This must be my excuse for the very full account I have felt bound to give, in the next chapter, of my own personal relations with Dick. The Dick I knew was among my dearest personal friends over a long period of years; but I am very far from claiming that I was his closest friend. Many others doubtless knew him better than I did; but I think that no one could have loved him, or had cause to love him, more deeply than I. The Dean of St Paul's, in his address at Dick's funeral service at St Paul's, told us that when he heard of Dick's death he said, "A light seems to have gone from the sky." That is exactly what I felt as I heard the news over the wireless. I had known him and loved him, and been loved by him, for so many years, in health as well as in sickness; in the days when he was so triumphantly carrying into reality his great vision of what St Martin's might be to the people of London; in the brightest as well as in the darkest days of his lovely and Christ-inspired life.

2

Dick as I Knew Him

MY acquaintance with Dick began in the year 1907. I had then just returned from five years' work in the Bush of New South Wales, where I had helped my friend the Reverend F. H. Campion to found the Brotherhood of the Good Shepherd, a society of young priests and laymen working in the huge "out-back" areas of that state. I was eager to get men to volunteer for that work and with that end in view I visited various theological colleges to describe the work and, if possible, to enlist recruits. Among the colleges I visited was Cuddesdon, and after addressing the students there I asked any one who was prepared to consider the possibility of going out to work in the Bush to come and see me privately. I was disappointed when only one man responded to my invitation, and I remember expressing my disappointment to the then principal, Canon Johnston. "Who is your one volunteer?" he asked, and when I told him it was a man called Sheppard, he said, "Well, at all events you have got by far the best man in the college." Dick was never allowed to go out to that work, or any other work overseas—except for his brief period of service as a chaplain in the first world-war and occasional journeys to preach in America—for he was too urgently needed for work in the Church at home. But from that time onward we were friends. It was not, however, till the birth of the so-called Life and Liberty Movement, in 1917, that we were thrown into close co-operation with one another.

The late Archbishop of Canterbury (William Temple) wrote soon after Dick's death of his work in connection with "Life and Liberty":

> "Apart from Dick Sheppard," he says, "there would have been no Life and Liberty Movement. In that sense

it was his creation; yet it was never, I think, quite what he wanted it to be. He conceived a movement for a great quickening of religion in the Church. As he discussed this with his friends he came to think that some loosening of legal bonds was necessary as a preliminary. So he agreed that our first point of concentration should be the Enabling Bill as proposed by Lord Selborne's Commission on Church and State, which had reported just before this stirring had begun. But it rather irked him, I think, that our objective should be the passing of an act of Parliament; and he was certainly not happy about the Assembly to which by that act Parliament gave certain powers. So, though he created the movement, and most loyally supported it, he did not seem to find in it the wholly appropriate channel for his energies—as I think he did in his own Peace Pledge Union.

"Yet the debt of the movement to him was incalculable—not only for existence but for quality. Our object was to secure an act of Parliament, but we never felt in the least degree like a political party or agitation. Our meetings were marked by intense and delightful fellowship. Of this the chief source was Dick himself. He assented to our policy, but for that he had little enthusiasm. He always looked beyond it. And so he kept us true in some measure to our own ideals. He gave to Life and Liberty—not its name, which came from Dr David, nor its first objective which was provided by Lord Selborne's Commission—but its existence and its special quality. If we think rather of the movement itself than of its goal, then he, more than anyone else, *was* the movement."

That seems to me to be a very just estimate of Dick's part in the Life and Liberty Movement. His one desire then, as through all the years that followed, was that the spirit of life and of liberty should be reborn in the Church, which seemed to him, and to many other ardent souls, to be, if not moribund, at least sadly lacking in vitality; and to be so fettered by tradition as to be almost incapable of any true adventure.

But though the movement eventually bitterly disappointed many of those whom in the beginning it had filled with high hopes, its early days were indeed full of enthusiasm. It was in those days that I first really got to know Dick and to share his mind. And it is perhaps worth recording here that it was after attending a Life and Liberty conference at High Leigh that an incident happened which might well have ended Dick's labours and my own in the Church Militant here on earth.

The conference had ended late on a Friday evening and as Dick was eager to get back to St Martin's as early as possible next morning, and I had to leave equally early to get back to St Peter's-in-Thanet for a wedding, I offered to drop Dick at St Martin's vicarage on my way through London. We made so early a start that there was almost no traffic about as we drove into London. It had been raining very lightly, just enough to make the streets greasy. All went well until we were just emerging from St Martin's Lane, when I perceived simultaneously that the road from the vicarage to the corner was up, so that our approach to the vicarage was barred by a rope enclosing a deep chasm, and that a large lorry, no doubt on its way to Covent Garden, was hurtling down upon us from the direction of Leicester Square, the driver no doubt taking advantage of the emptiness of the streets to go "all out". It looked as though a collision was unavoidable. I turned to the left hoping that the lorry would hit us on the slant, rather than broadside on, and at the same time instinctively jammed on my brakes. The lorry-driver jammed on his. We both skidded, and I came to a stop with one wheel over the abyss, facing a sweet shop at the corner of the square. The lorry skidded much more violently and came to rest a foot behind my car, but facing in the direction from which it had been coming. Dick and I agreed that it was one of the most terrifying experiences of our lives. He wrote to me on the Monday a highly characteristic note, saying that he had told his people of the adventure, and that he had made up his mind that we were both of us doomed and that his only regret was that he was to die smashing in the front of an inoffensive sweet-shop rather than knocking down that artistic abomination, the Cavell memorial!

§

When, a year or two later, Dick carried into effect his dream of creating an entirely new type of parish magazine, *St Martin's Review*, he wrote and asked me to contribute some light articles, which I was glad to do. Some of these I illustrated and my namesake, the Reverend H. J. Matthews, who was then on the staff of St Martin's, told me that St Martin's folk credited him with all my contributions and his fellow-curate, the Reverend Ronald Sinclair—a far better cartoonist than I ever was—with all my drawings. I can only hope that neither of their reputations was permanently blotted by my indiscretions. The Review was always a joy to those who, like myself, had no use for the ordinary parish magazine. I contributed to it regularly during Dick's and Pat McCormick's editorships, and on one occasion, at Dick's urgent request, I wrote a leading article on The Unimportance of the Important. We both of us felt very strongly that bishops attached far too much importance to the opinions of the titled and wealthy members of the Church, an importance which seemed to us to be far from the mind of the Church's Founder.

An incident occurred in the late summer of 1921 which is perhaps worth recording as evidence of the immense attraction of Dick's name by that time. He had promised to come and preach in my church, St Peter's, in the Isle of Thanet. I had let my vicarage and was living in a little cottage, without a telephone. Dick was advertised to preach at Evensong, and just before the hour of the service a message reached me from a parishioner who lived some distance from the church to say that Mrs Sheppard had rung him up and asked him to let me know that Dick had been seized with sudden illness after taking the morning service at St Martin's, and had been forbidden to attempt the journey to Thanet. When I went over to my church I found it already packed to the doors, and an enormous queue of others trying to get in. Inside they were sitting on the step of the sanctuary and standing wherever there was room to stand. It was horrible to have to announce before the service began that Dick could not come. But the exit of a large part of the congregation, which I had expected to follow the announcement, did not take place, and when the time for the sermon arrived I just got up into the pulpit and told the people all I knew about Dick's work at St Martin's and the secret of his success—his whole-hearted love for our Lord and for all his fellowmen. The congregation, no doubt sympathizing with me in the predicament in which I found myself, and far more with Dick in his illness, were plainly in a mood to turn even their disappointment to good.

§

Early in the following year I myself became desperately ill. Double pneumonia, with various complications, left me, after many weeks in bed, with an abscess on the lung and the doctors in doubt as to whether my heart was strong enough to stand up to an operation. I was forbidden to have any visitors except my wife, but when Dick rang her up one day to ask if he could see me in the nursing home to which I had been removed, my doctor, who knew Dick, said that an exception might be made in his case. I have the most vivid memory of that visit. The door of my room opened and Dick tip-toed in, took my hand in his and greeted me. Then he knelt down and remained in silent prayer for some time. Then he rose from his knees, pressed my hand and turned to leave the room. I remember blurting out, between the incessant and painful bouts of coughing, "Don't go, Dick!" "Shan't I tire you too much, if I stay?" asked Dick. "No, Dick, *you* will never tire me." "Can you stand a funny story?" "I can stand anything from you, Dick." So he told me, in his own inimitable way, a story of how the great Monsieur Coué, who had just been having a tremendous reception in London, had been asked by some of Dick's friends to cure him of his asthma and insomnia. So, for fourteen nights running the good M. Coué came and glared at Dick from the foot of his bed, and repeated over and over again, "My boy, you are ver' sleepy, ver' sleepy, ver' sleepy. . . ." And then, "You are almost asleep. . . ." And finally a triumphant, "You *are* asleep! . . ." "By which time," said Dick, "I felt more wide-awake than ever before in my life." The "cure," though quite ineffective, had a most amusing sequel, which I cannot here report; but Dick's telling of it reduced me to uncontrollable laughter, which in its turn provoked such a violent fit of coughing that I burst the abscess on my lung, with the result that soon after Dick's departure I had a complete collapse, from which I came to to find two doctors and three nurses round my bed, pumping oxygen into me through brandy—and from that moment I began to get better.

The whole incident, as I look back upon it, seems somehow so entirely characteristic of Dick. Who but Dick would have made the time, in the midst of a life so overfull of important work, to journey from London to Broadstairs and back to try to help one sick friend? Who combined as he did such profound and simple religious feeling with the most glorious sense of humour and pure fun—so that he could pass, in a moment, quite naturally from the grave to the gay without arousing any sense of incongruity in the minds of those who were with him?

I think it was this visit to me which made Dick choose this same nursing home in Broadstairs as his refuge when, some years later, he was forced to undergo one of his all too numerous "cures," after a bad breakdown in London. It was in fact a very remarkable home, in that it was run by a friend and parishioner of mine who as a result of some unnecessary and badly bungled surgery had been himself compelled to spend long bouts of time in various nursing homes, and had resolved, if ever he got well enough to do so, to turn his experience to good account by starting a nursing home which should be free from all the unnecessary discomforts he had had to endure in those he had been confined in. It was, in fact, as nearly the ideal nursing home as possible.

But at the time of his visit to me Dick was himself in comparatively good health, and after my return from a long convalescence he came down to Broadstairs to open a new hall which we had built in my parish. It was a great occasion for us. Naturally the hall was packed, and among other local notables on the platform was the then Mayor of Ramsgate, seated in the front and wearing an immaculate pair of white spats. When it was Dick's turn to speak, he shuffled forward to the front of the platform and stood with one foot curled over the other. Then he turned to me and said, 'Mr. Chairman, I have just made a terrible discovery. In the front of one of my socks there is a large hole! Now at last I think I have discovered why distinguished people, dukes and earls and mayors and such-like, wear spats!" And from that introduction he passed on to a perfect sketch of the possible uses of such a hall as ours in the life of a parish.

In the following year (1923) Dick went to America for the first time. He received innumerable requests for sermons from American parsons, and I remember him telling me with immense amusement about one such invitation. Knowing nothing about the parson who had sent it, he wrote to the bishop of his diocese to find out what he could about this man and his church before replying to the invitation. The bishop, Dick said, evidently thought of St Martin's as, at all events possibly, a centre of "stunts." (This, of course, it never was. Dick loathed "stunts" and those who accused him of being a "stunt-merchant"—and there were such among clergy, envious of a success they could never themselves earn—never had any justification for the charge.) So the bishop wrote in answer to Dick's enquiries something to this effect: "We over here think this clergyman's methods somewhat bizarre—though perhaps they may not seem so to you. For instance, whenever he mentions 'hell' in his sermons—which he does with considerable frequency—he touches a button in the pulpit, which causes a trap-door in the nave to fly open, whence flames leap up in the middle of the church. Another of his practices which seems to us a little *outré* is to have a company of young women dancing ballets in the sanctuary in honour of the Blessed Virgin." Dick did not accept the invitation to preach in that church, and that visit to America was a very great disappointment. He fell ill with influenza directly he arrived there, and was ill all the rest of the visit.

§

It was in 1926 that Dick came back to Cliffe Coombe Nursing Home at Broadstairs; this time as a patient. During the many months that followed I was brought into very intimate contact with him. Very soon after his arrival, when I myself was on a brief visit to London, I was rung up by Mrs Sheppard to say that Dick wanted me to broadcast at St Martin's instead of him, as the doctors had forbidden him to attempt it. I returned to St Peter's next day, and went at once to see Dick and ask him if he wanted me to preach on any particular subject. "Tell them," he said, in effect, "to believe in the God revealed in Jesus Christ; not in their Old Testament God of wrath and of battles." That sermon of mine gave me a deeper insight than I could otherwise have had into what his broadcast sermons cost Dick. I remember the flood of letters which reached me from all over the British Isles and even from the middle of France—letters which it took me three weeks to answer. Later on Dick told me that usually while he was at St Martin's he sat up two whole nights a week answering letters which came to him as a result of his broadcast sermons.

In this connection I should like to record one characteristic act of Dick's. One of my sons, on holiday one summer at a seaside village in Cornwall, lodged in the house of an old blacksmith, whose greatest joy in life was to listen to Dick's broadcasts. The old man told my son how he had determined at last to take a week-end ticket to London, that he might see as well as hear his beloved preacher. He got to St Martin's half-an-hour before the service was due to begin, thinking that would be time enough, but when he got there the church was already packed to the doors and people were being turned away. So the old man returned home without having seen Dick. It was, he said, the bitterest disappointment of his life. I wrote to Dick and told him the old man's story. Dick replied by return of post asking my son to send him the old man's address, that he might write to him himself. It is easy to imagine the joy of the old blacksmith when that letter from his beloved preacher arrived.

Of Dick's ministry at St Martin's it is really unnecessary to write here. I was very frequently at the church during those fruitful years and I saw something of the catholicity of Dick's appeal to men and women. Kings and commoners, dukes and dustmen, countesses and charwomen, men and women with all kinds of backgrounds and very different outlooks upon life, attended the great church and loved, and felt they were loved by, their vicar. When he was known to be desperately ill, crowds came to pray for him at all hours of the day and night. No wonder Dick had a vision of what the Church might be everywhere, if only its leaders would break away from musty traditionalism and pre-occupation with matters of ecclesiastical politics, and really "seek first the Kingdom of God and his righteousness," on fire with his Spirit—the Spirit of love. No wonder he became more and more convinced that the Enabling Act, to the passing of which the members of the Life and Liberty Movement had devoted so much precious time, had brought no new life, and no liberty worthy of the name, to those who, like him, were concerned not with external organization but with multitudes of hungry souls, untended and unfed.

Dick in the nursing home at Broadstairs created problems for others as well as for himself. His doctor had, not for the first or last time, ordered him the complete rest, of which he was in such obvious need. A request was published that he should be spared all letters. Only a chosen few were given his address. He was to have no visitors. I myself went to see him only at his own urgent request and with the approval of his doctor. It was a joy to be allowed to celebrate Holy Communion from time to time in his room. But in spite of all precautions his whereabouts gradually leaked out. Letters, usually marked 'urgent' or 'private,' began to arrive in increasing numbers. People began to turn up at the nursing home who had never even troubled to find out beforehand whether their visits would be welcome, saying that they had come all the way from London on urgent matters. And Dick—being what he was—would not allow them to be sent away without seeing him. Often he pressed bank notes into their hands before they left: "It was so good of you to come and see me. I just couldn't bear to think of you being put to all this expense on my behalf." Once when I myself had been hurriedly sent for by him and had had to take a taxi to get to the home, Dick spotted the taxi from the window of his room and said, "I can't have you taking taxis at your own expense, Charlie. Nurse, give Mr Matthews a ten-shilling note from my drawer"; and when I refused it he got so excited that I had for his sake to accept it, and return it surreptitiously to the nurse to be put back in his drawer.

But what more than anything else made any real rest or recuperation impossible during the more than seven months that he remained in the nursing home was the problem of the future of his beloved St Martin's. He knew that he could not carry on any longer at the impossible pace he had set himself. What was to happen to his dear church and people?

I was deeply involved in this problem; first, because Dick himself asked me if I would be ready to accept the living if it were to be offered to me; and, secondly, because the then archdeacon of London, the Venerable E. E. Holmes, who frequently came down to Thanet and sometimes attended the services in St Peter's, asked me to come and talk over with him the whole question of the future of St Martin's. Both the archdeacon and Dick were terrified lest a certain priest, who was what Dick, as I have said, was not, a theatrical "stunt-merchant," should be offered the living by the bishop of London (Dr Winnington-Ingram), whose judgement of men was by no means always infallible. A rumour that his appointment was contemplated had somehow got abroad and the bishop himself was at that time on a visit to the Far East. The archdeacon wanted to know whether I would accept the post if it were offered. Being profoundly conscious that I could never hope to do what Dick had done, I made the alternative suggestion that I should join the staff of St Martin's as a sort of understudy to Dick, with a view to relieving him of as much work and worry as possible, while Dick himself remained vicar. All I felt able to promise, if he refused to stay on, was that I would not refuse the job without very earnest consideration. It was therefore without any "pang," but rather with intense relief and gratitude, that I read the letter I received from Dick, undated, but written, I think in September 1926:—

"Dearest Charlie,

"I have just heard news and if it gives you even a momentary pang I shall be broken-hearted—I got it by the second post. You know, I think, that I invited a committee of 10 glorious fellows and 2 women, from my P.C.C. to meet me here and discuss my successor. I had over 300 applicants or folk recommended, and before they came I eliminated 200 impossible folk leaving 100 in for the meeting of the Committee in this room. In five minutes we eliminated 94 leaving you [and five others whom he names]. I spoke to them about each and shewed no preference. I told them I would accept gladly any candidate they named except 2 of them whom I did not think suitable and that if they chose one of those two I should ask them to give me a chance of influencing their judgement. As I told you beforehand I did not think it was my business to put pressure on them for it is they who will have to rejoice or repent my successor. They went away and unanimously chose Pat, whom as far as I know they know next to nothing about. . . . I love my Pat, as you do, and think any parish would be lucky to have him."

For myself, the knowledge that Dick would have welcomed me as his successor at St Martin's remains the greatest honour I have ever received, an honour of which I wish I could think myself worthy.

§

Next year, 1927, saw the publication of *The Impatience of a Parson*. Of that book I shall have to write in a subsequent chapter. I will only say here that I was quite convinced from the first that Dick's fear, expressed in letters from his sickbed to Maude Royden and others, and made, I think, much too much of by Mr Ellis Roberts, that there would be no further job offered to him in the Church of England after its publication, was really groundless. First, because I could not believe that that fate could befall the man who had done more than any other to make, not only the particular church he served, but church-life all over the country a vital force in the nation's life. The bishops, though no doubt some among them would shake their heads over Dick's rebelliousness and murmur to one another, in private, "Poor Dick Sheppard! It is a pity his heart is so much better than his head!," would never dare to inhibit him even if they wished to do so. And secondly, more than ten years before *The Impatience of a Parson* appeared I had myself edited and largely written, in conjunction with several other rebels, some of them Dick's close friends, two perhaps even more rebellious books, both of which had a wide circulation at the time; and though they had indeed been frowned upon by many bishops, and I had shared Dick's fear in regard to my own position, I had in fact been allowed to continue my own ministry in the Church.

Dick often told me that he owed a great deal to these two books, *Faith or Fear?* and *Faith and Freedom*, and indeed he quotes passages from them in *The Impatience of a Parson* and *If I Were Dictator*, and it was, no doubt, this feeling which appears in some of the letters he wrote to me. When, for instance, Maude Royden had told him that I had written a long and favourable review of his book in *The Church of England Newspaper*, he wrote, "Beloved Charlie, Maude Royden has just told me that you wrote such a generous review of my little book. . . . Oh Charlie I am *grateful*. You see you said these things years ago & were my teacher. . . ." And the next day came another letter: "Since I wrote last night I have read, with more happiness than I can possibly tell you, your review of my book. I often wondered, dearest old man, what you would think of it and feared greatly that you might be obliged to sum up against me, and yet I remembered that you had years ago gone for the things I am feebly striving after now. I do thank God, not merely that you agree with me, but that I can, now I have read the review, feel that the book was worth while. I shan't mind now being damned by the critics. Charles, I thank you with all my heart for what you have taught me." And to this letter there was a postscript, "Can't we go butting about together one day with Jacks and Gray and others?"

That Dick's fears for his future in the Church of England were needless was conclusively shown when in 1929 he was made dean of Canterbury. On that occasion he wrote to me:—

"My dearest Charlie,
"I can't let you read news of me in the paper. After a lot of thought I have accepted the Deanery of Canterbury, but the point of this letter is to tell you, before God, that I feel exactly like a boy who has got a prize by cribbing from you and about two others. Alas! if I owned up it wouldn't help, but when I see you Charles

and G.E.M. [my wife] please know how utterly humble I shall feel in your presence; Your always loving

DICK."

Dick's stay at Canterbury was all too brief—only two years—and as I left the Canterbury diocese to become Chaplain of Marlborough College very soon after his appointment, I had no personal knowledge of his work there; but of what he accomplished in those two years the following account sent to me by his friend, and mine, Mr J. McClemens, who was at that time senior vesturer and sub-sacrist, gives a graphic and touching picture.

> "During those two wonderful years of our beloved Dick at Canterbury," writes Mr McClemens, "he was away very ill more than once. He got to love the great and gloriously beautiful cathedral passionately and formed lovely plans for its future use by all kinds of people. He made himself familiar with all the statutes, ancient and modern . . . he loved grand music, beautiful and quiet ceremonial. But he cared little for gorgeous robes or unnecessary 'fal-de-lals'. . . . He used to enter the cathedral at all hours of the night, with his little torch in his hand. This habit at first startled the night-watchman, but he soon got used to seeing his dean kneeling in front of one of the altars in silent prayer. Dick, when he got up, would greet him warmly, saying 'I hope you will forgive me for disturbing you.' The man used to report these visits to me, as it was his duty to tell me of anything that happened during his time on duty. The cathedral cleaners, who came on duty at 6 a.m. in summer and 7 a.m. in winter, would often find him there when they arrived and he always greeted them warmly and would enquire about their wives and children. If any of them had illness or other

trouble at home, his great and generous heart always saw to it that they were helped in the most practical way. And all this without fuss of any kind. He seemed to hate even being thanked. I was his almoner in many acts of love.

"His name was a magnet. Many thousands visited the cathedral all the year round just in the hope that they might see him, speak to him, or hear him read a lesson. When he was announced to preach people came from all parts, hours before the service was timed to begin. The cathedral was thronged. and I had to have the doors closed. His sermons exhausted him. He gave his all. The huge congregations were thrilled by his preaching and his personality. There was nothing academic in his sermons. He used the simplest words that all could understand. In all my forty-five years of listening to the greatest preachers and teachers in the Church of England I have never seen anyone approach him in his power of stirring men's souls. I remember a congregation of over 2,000 men of the British Legion stirred alternately to laughter and to tears as they hung upon his words. His influence upon all sorts and conditions of men and women was touching to behold. Despite all his suffering he was full of life, and full of fun and gaiety and he loved to see others happy. What was the secret of his power? It was, in one word, Christ. He loved Christ. He taught Christ and men came to see Christ in him—our redeemer and our friend. And how Christ-like he was in his understanding of men, women and little children. You could not deceive Dick. He could sum up and see through everyone. Here too he was like his Master. Though exhausted by his preaching he would nevertheless insist on going down to the south-west door and shaking hands with all who wished to do so.

"One day Dick and I came out of the treasury and found a lot of men, obviously miners, standing looking at the chained Bible. Dick immediately welcomed them warmly, shook hands with them all and asked if they had seen all the cathedral. When they said 'No,' Dick turned to me and said, 'Here is my friend who will show you all our treasures.' They looked mystified, obviously not knowing who he was. I said, 'This is the Dean of Canterbury, the head of the cathedral, but you will know him best as Dick Sheppard.' Smiles appeared on all their faces and broadened when Dick said, 'Yes. I am the boss here now.' They did not know much about deans but they knew what a boss was.

"One sad day Mrs Sheppard sent for me. She was in great distress. She told me that Dick was determined to resign and begged me to try to persuade him to change his mind. I told her that Dick had already told me of his intention and I had done my best to persuade him to reconsider his decision, but I would try again. It was all in vain. He was adamant. 'I am ill,' he said, 'I keep on getting ill. I must go.' When he was first made dean he seemed to be in excellent health, but now he was a physical wreck. A cathedral chapter was really no place for him. He needed a whole cathedral to himself, untrammelled, alone in authority. But if he had no great admiration for ecclesiastical authorities in general, he greatly loved, and was loved by, his spiritual father, Archbishop Lang. You could not help loving Dick. As Edward Woods, now bishop of Lichfield, once said to me, walking down the nave of the cathedral, 'hundreds of years elapse between the coming of a St Francis, a Savonarola and a Dick Sheppard. For he was a revolutionary, in the same sense that Christ himself was a revolutionary. He hated all sham and humbug.

"I must conclude these memories of Canterbury days with two more incidents, trivial in themselves perhaps, but characteristic of Dick's thoughtfulness for others. When it was known that the archbishop was attending a service, the dean would go to the Old Palace, preceded by his verger with the mace. While waiting for the archbishop, Dick would say to me, 'You must sit down. You are an older man than I am.' One day when he and I were walking through the cloisters we met a cathedral workman. Dick greeted him and offered him a cigarette from his case. The man took it and thanked him, but said that he was not allowed to smoke while on duty. That man, as I happen to know, treasured that cigarette to his dying day. Dick loved me from the first because I had known and loved his father, Dr Edgar Sheppard, sub-dean of the Chapels Royal."

I have quoted this little tribute of Mr McClemens in full because it reveals so simply and directly the impact of Dick's personality on 'the common man,' whose century this is said to be. "I loved him; he loved me." How many men and women have said that of Dick and said it quite truly! Indeed I wonder if any Christian priest down the ages has loved and been loved by a greater number or a greater variety of people.

§

For the next few years after I left the Canterbury diocese I only saw Dick at very rare intervals. But I kept in touch with him, in spite of the fact that, having seen while I was at Broadstairs something of the volume of his correspondence, I made a self-denying ordinance that I would never write to him unless he first wrote to me. This he did, however, fairly frequently, usually to ask my help, which I was always delighted to give. For instance, towards the end of 1930 I had an urgent letter from him saying that the B.B.C. was insisting on his giving a broadcast talk in a series on science and religion. He knew that I had taken my degree in science and he wrote, "I know no science and if you would write my talk for me I should be eternally grateful," and he added characteristically, "Of course I shall send you the fee." I agreed to do this and when I sent him my paper he wrote a note saying, "It is exactly right. You won't mind if I just add one or two little sentences of my own."

In 1935 Dick came to stay at our house at Fyfield, near Marlborough, and revisited the college at which years before he had been so desperately unhappy. He preached in the school chapel and spoke to the Scout troop of the college. That visit was, as Mr Roberts himself records, "a huge success." On that occasion Dick gave to me, and also to the then master of Marlborough, Mr G. C. Turner, versions of his unhappy experiences as a boy strangely different from the account which Mr Roberts quotes in his Life. My own belief is that the form-master whose treatment of Dick was the root cause of his sad experience at the college was indeed guilty of what I myself, as an old schoolmaster and school chaplain, would agree is one of the most grievous mistakes of which any schoolmaster can be guilty: the mistake of speaking sarcastically to a small boy. Boys never understand sarcasm. It hurts them more than their elders seem to realize, and they hate it. That Dick's form-master was guilty of this grievous error I can well believe. But I do not think that anyone studying the portrait of this particular master, as I have done, and knowing how greatly beloved he was by many of his boys, could believe him to be the sadistic monster of Mr Roberts's imagination.

Be that as it may. It was an enormous happiness to me to

c

be, in part at least, responsible for bringing back Dick to his old school, so short a time, alas! before his death, and to know that that visit gave him great happiness.

Only a few days before this was written a present housemaster of Marlborough was speaking to me of the great impression Dick made on the Scouts by the simple little address he gave to them on the secret he knew so well of true joy. He said that the letters of that word "joy," taken in their own order, really revealed the secret: "J"—Jesus first; "O"—Other people next; and "Y"—Yourself, last. Rather childish, you say, perhaps? Say rather childlike; and remember what Jesus said about becoming as little children. The boys who heard that address, I will wager, will remember it when they have forgotten all the learned orations of the great preachers who visited their chapel in their schooldays.

I cannot remember whether I ever met Dick again after that happy visit. I called on him once, later on, at Amen Court, but he was out; and of course he wrote a characteristic note: "I am sorry I missed you, beloved Charles. God bless you all for Christmas and for ever—Your loving Dick."

During the time that Dick concentrated upon his Peace Pledge Union campaign I saw little of him. It was a real grief to me that, for reasons which will appear in a later chapter, I could never join that movement, though I had actually, at his request, contributed a series of articles, "In the Cause of Peace," to *St Martin's Review*. But our difference of opinion never for one moment clouded our friendship. I could never understand those, of whom there were many, who had called themselves his friends, and yet because of his pacifism felt it necessary to cold-shoulder him.

One other thing must be said about the sad days when Dick was in Harrogate, after the great tragedy which clouded the end of his life had fallen upon him. Mr Roberts in his book speaks as though he were the only friend of Dick who visited him, or tried to help him. This was really not the fact. Dick was not an easy person to help. He preferred to bear his own burdens rather than call upon others, however willing, to share them. But one, at least, of Dick's oldest friends and colleagues of St Martin's days, the Rev H. L. Johnston, had hastened to his aid at Harrogate before ever Mr Roberts went there at all. And this leads me to say that in my judgement Mr Roberts in his chapter on St Martin-in-the-Fields does far too little justice to Dick's two greatest helpers of those days, Hugo Johnston and Charles Ritchie, who again and again kept the flag flying when Dick was away ill. Mr Ritchie reveals one of the secrets of the loyal devotion which Dick inspired in his colleagues at St Martin's when he says that Dick invited him to come and work *with* him: not *under* him, as so many vicars would say to their prospective curates. I should like to record here my immense admiration for the loyal and self-suppressing way in which these two kept Dick's spirit alive in the church and parish of St Martin's, in extremely difficult circumstances.

3

At St Martin-in-the-Fields

I DO not think that it can be doubted that Dick Sheppard's greatest contribution to the religious life of England was in what he first dreamed of, and later so wonderfully realized at St Martin-in-the-Fields. And let it be said at once that the whole life of St Martin's centred in, and radiated from, the worship at the altar. He found a church, when he came to it in 1914, in which a tiny handful of people worshipped, in a rather drab atmosphere and a fashion that lacked the true light and colour of worship. He made of that church first and foremost a real home for thousands and thousands of people, who first learned there what it meant to be children of the God who is love; who had become fired, as their pastor and friend was himself fired, with love for Jesus Christ; people for whom worship had become a thing of joy and beauty, an inspiration to a life of service. It is the simple truth that the services at St Martin's inspired hundreds of clergy up and down the country with a new vision of what a parish church might be.

Men with the minds of the Scribes and Pharisees used to sneer at Dick. They used to say that his success was a purely "personal" success: that men were attracted by his "personality," as though that were something to be ashamed of. Is it not one of the very lessons of the incarnation of God in Jesus Christ that it is just through a wholly consecrated personality that God saves men? Was it not the "personality" of St Paul, created by his own personal love for the Lord of whom he could say "He loved me, and gave himself for me," which made him the greatest missionary the world has ever known? Was it not the consecrated "personality" of Francis of Assisi that attracted to him disciples who could turn the world of their day upside down? And is not the secret of true life-giving "personality" always the same—that all the instincts, all the gifts and potentialities of the individual are subordinate to, or organized round, the central integrating, passion of love?

"If," he wrote (and the passage I quote is in my judgement the finest he ever wrote), "if the disciple can maintain a constant conversation with his Lord, the greatest of all gifts will inevitably be his. It will be as natural for him to love as to breathe." And then, after a characteristic aside on the distressing character of what he calls the "official love" of those clergy and church workers who "seem to have determined that it is part of their professional duty to love, and so they love because they must," he goes on:

> "Love in its highest manifestation is the richest, most persuasive, loveliest, nicest thing God has to offer—it is the only weapon we need. It is full of understanding—it knows how easy it is to sin, how difficult to live nobly. It sees with the eyes of those it loves. It never makes quick, harsh judgements. It gets to the heart of a situation as nothing else. It thinks in terms of men and women and children, and never in terms of 'hands' or statistics. It prefers to give itself to the individual. It shuns expression on public platforms. It has no ulterior object except to serve. It would gladly lead if it could—it would never drive. It asks nothing for itself, but it is human enough to long for love in return. It knows when to speak and when to be silent, when to be patient and when to be impatient. It is at home with all sorts and conditions of men and women and children, and it makes them laugh, for it has a real vein of humour. It gives and gets a joy in loving. It believes in all men and women. There is no such word as

'hopeless' within its vocabulary. It feels; it is sensitive to the moods of all to whom it is given. It is never clumsy, and yet it often steps in where angels fear to tread. Perhaps its greatest characteristic is its power to understand. It anticipates man's needs; it can see a situation sometimes before it occurs; it has an almost superhuman instinct for what ought to be done and how to do it. It knows what is in the heart of man. It is not always declaring itself. Like all creative forces, its best work is done in quietness. It prefers action to speech, it would prefer to visit someone in want to making any oration on fellowship. It likes best to do small things that no one else has seen need doing. It sees sorrow where sorrow is thought to be hidden, and virtue and grandeur where it is least expected. It is for ever on the watch for those who need it. It runs to give itself as the father ran to the prodigal son, not because he pitied, but because he could not do without his son. It washes the disciples' feet as He did because it wants to—not because there is a lesson in humility to be taught. It is like a window through which can be heard all the cries of the market-place without. It knows no barrier of rank or class, of creed or colour. It overflows the boundary of its own denomination—no official channels can hold it entirely. It flows, perhaps, most tenderly to those who never enter church and care little for the love of God. It sees the crown of their need on their foreheads and longs to be of service.

"It is always courteous, especially to women. It knows that He who is love had a mother; it recognizes that, save for the faith and moral courage of women, it would indeed have gone hard with his cause. It suffers no slighting thing to be said of them: it respects them too much. It grieves and is silent when they fail. It is courteous—this love—to older people and quite young people too. It likes them to say what they feel. It enters a slum dwelling with as much respect as it enters the lordly mansion. It could not patronize if it tried—it understands too much. It is generous, yet strong in controversy. It seeks to win without wounding—it never descends to personal abuse or bitter speech. It is sometimes angry, for there is nothing sickly or sentimental about it. It is never shocked. When it is angry it is because another is hurt—in soul, or mind, or body. It knows nothing of jealousy—it rejoices in another's success. It is never petty or mean. It has all things in their right proportion. It is ever seeking to disentangle itself from irrelevancies.

"It learns more in listening than in speech. It is never sarcastic, for it knows that by such means no soul was ever won. It is the property of no clique—it wears no ecclesiastical badge. It cares nothing for its own status —there is nothing professional about it. It is not always trying to buy up the opportunity, to point the lesson and draw the moral. Above all, its faith in God is massive. It is confident always that in the end darkness must flee before light. This love which comes of God through Jesus Christ is the one weapon we need. If we who are to serve in the Society of Christ could possess it from constant conversation with our Lord, we shall not have lived in vain.

"Men who see it will know from whence it comes, and they will give praise to God who can do such great things. They will know also why we are what we are and what are the essentials of Christianity."

I have quoted that passage in full, because it explains for me all that Dick accomplished in the thirteen years he spent at St Martin's. Some men think of that work in terms of popular services, with the Guards' band to play the music;

clubs for the button-boys of the hotels in the neighbourhood, a crypt open by night to the "down-and-outs," wonderful organization, inspired "publicity," Christmas appeals, and a hundred other things, which all helped to make the church a centre of overflowing life and fellowship.

St Martin's was all this; but it was so very much more. It was a church where men learned to worship with full hearts the God of love, whom so many of them had first come to believe in at St Martin's, not only from the words, but even more from the deeds of its beloved vicar. Hundreds who came there first out of curiosity to see for themselves what this odd young parson was really like were converted by the love which flowed from him continually, ever renewed from that hidden source, where he himself maintained "a constant conversation with his Lord."

Dick Sheppard's ministry at St Martin's was indeed a personal ministry; but that through the love of him—the "brother whom they had seen"—men were led to love "the God whom they had not seen," was abundantly proved by the fact that when, as happened all too often, he was away from St Martin's for long periods through ill-health the work there went on just the same. The church was crowded to the doors and its family life—for Dick had made the church a real home for hundreds of folk—flourished. And in that church his influence abides today, as its present vicar testifies, though it is so many years since he ministered there. And up and down the country there are many other churches where the services are marked by a greater reality, the worship of God is more vital, because of what Dick did at St Martin's between 1914 and 1927.

4

Was He a Revolutionary?

Mr Ellis Roberts, in his life of Dick Sheppard is at pains to show that Dick was not in fact a revolutionary at all. He writes (p. 87):

"He was not an innovator: he made old things new. He was not an inventor: he gave to reverently preserved things new and startling life. In his heart he was a man of much sad doubt, timid, self-distrustful; but he lived Love. He had too little patience, and too little self-discipline, but where other priests can give us the fruits of their patience, the lessons of their discipline, Dick gave his life. The church of St Martin-in-the-Fields, as Dick made it, was a great Lover's gift to London." Again (p. 111): "No one can understand those twelve years at St Martin-in-the-Fields who does not recognize the truth that H. R. L. Sheppard was a man with old-fashioned ideas who was eager to try new-fashioned methods to get the ideas across."

And, commenting on Dick's suggestions for the reforms he thought necessary if St Paul's was really to become, what he longed that it should become, a living centre of the religious life of London, a great central church of the people, its chapter really in vital touch with ordinary men and women, its members eschewing their dignified isolation from the roaring life of the metropolis, Mr Roberts writes: "Such extravagant statements have occasionally been made about Dick's revolutionary ideas that it seemed best to quote [the passages in which Dick himself expressed his desired reforms. See p. 49 below] in evidence of how little a rebel he was." And finally, of Dick's campaign for pacifism

Mr Roberts writes, "The growth of official disapprobation distressed him. Never a natural rebel, never rejoicing in opposition, he became even more sensitive when his views on war met with disapproval from those in authority" (p. 295).

With all that Mr Roberts says on this question I find myself in substantial agreement. Dick was not what most men mean by a revolutionary. He had an innate reverence for what is old, a very deep appreciation of the great heritage bequeathed to the world by the past. He was never more at home anywhere than in the glorious cathedral at Canterbury, except perhaps in that at Chartres, to which he would flee from time to time from the bustle and clamour of London. And unlike so many revolutionaries he was never content to be merely destructive. He neither thought nor acted, as revolutionaries so often seem to think and act, as though God had been inactive in the past and was concerned only with the present and future. For him, at least in ecclesiastical matters, the path of true progress was the *via media*—the straight and narrow way between extremes. "Am I asking for revolution within the Church?" he asks almost wistfully, towards the end of *The Impatience of a Parson* (p. 228), and he answers his own question in these words, "Yes, I suppose so, but for one which is led by the leaders of the Church and especially by him who will preside at the next Lambeth Conference." And a little further on in the same chapter he writes, "I sincerely pray that reform may come from above and not proceed in an unauthorized manner from below—but come it must" (p. 232). These are not the utterances of a typical revolutionary. But then Dick was himself unique. He was never "typical" in anything he said or did.

And though the revolution he consciously sought to bring about, in the Church first, and later in the world outside the Church, never materialized in his own life-time, at least as he envisaged it—not one of the eighteen draft resolutions he hoped the Lambeth Conference would pass in 1930 was ever accepted, or I imagine, even considered, by the bishops—Dick's spirit still lives, and where it lives it does have a revolutionary effect on individuals and even on the Church at large.

Whether many people today read the books he published I greatly doubt. Some of them were unobtainable during the war years. But the fact that over 100,000 copies of *The Impatience of a Parson* were sold in his life-time is surely evidence of the appeal his pleas for reform made among his contemporaries.

But I believe that Mr Roberts's dictum that Dick was "a man with old-fashioned ideas, who was eager to try new methods to get those ideas across," if not the whole truth, is yet substantially justified. Dick recognized that a church was necessary for the conservation and propagation of the truth Jesus came to reveal. But he wanted a church more truly catholic than the historical church had ever yet been. And he believed that Dostoievsky's Legend of the Grand Inquisitor, in *The Brothers Karamazov*, was a true indictment, not only of the leaders of the Roman Church, but of those of his own branch of the Church. They would all of them, if they were honest and saw themselves as Christ saw them, have to make the awful confession to him, "We have corrected thy work." He wanted a church alive with the adventurous Spirit of his Master. He wanted also to retain, but in much simplified forms, the traditional offices of the Church. He believed, for instance, that the Church was right to welcome the little children into its fold by Baptism, but he wanted the baptismal office to be far simpler than that of the Revised Prayer Book of 1928. He rightly regarded the 1662 service of Baptism as almost unintelligible to the average layman. And the same is true of the marriage service and indeed all the occasional offices.

He loved the Eucharistic Service and I do not think he ever desired that that should be drastically altered, though into his own celebration of that service he was not afraid, as Canon Crum recorded in the account of Dick's time at Canterbury which he contributed after Dick's death to the memorial number of *St Martin's Review*, a note of human, as well as divine fellowship, which was surely in accordance with the mind of his Master. But if he did not want any drastic alteration of that service, he did most emphatically plead that everyone who loved the Lord Jesus sincerely should be admitted to the altar of the Church, to whatever denomination he might belong.

Here indeed he was a rebel. For him there was only one all-embracing Christian law, "Love, and do what you like." To the legalist and narrow traditionalist this patristic dictum[1] seems terribly dangerous; and dangerous it is to those who do not know what love really means, how terrific are the demands it makes, how the true "lover" can never "like" to do anything that will harm the neighbour whom he loves as himself. But in this respect Dick had no contemporary equal to himself. Love drove and consumed him. Ecclesiastical rules were no doubt necessary for the general welfare of the Church, but there were far too many of them; and too many were the result of the arbitrary translation of some of the sayings of Jesus into 'laws' which He never intended them to be. For Jesus laid down no 'laws' and the great saying, "The sabbath was made for man and not man for the sabbath" does reveal a universal principle, which applies to all ecclesiastical rules. Dick himself would have gone so far as to say, "The Church—with all its rules—was made for man, and not man for the Church."

When Dick, who was then a canon of St Paul's, was elected president of the undenominational Brotherhood

[1] The words are St Augustine's: *Comm. in Epist. Joannis*, tractatus vii, para. 8. (Migne *P.L.*, Vol. 35, p. 2003.)

Movement in 1934 he raised a storm among the legalists of his own church by officiating at a celebration of the Lord's Supper at Middlesbrough on the occasion of the movement's annual conference. He was violently denounced as a law-breaker by members of the narrowest sect of the Anglo-Catholics, men who though they feel themselves free to disregard any authority they happen to dislike, including that of the bishops to whom they have sworn canonical obedience, are unwilling to allow any freedom to those who do not share their own narrow and rigid outlook. These men roundly accused Dick of sacrilege, and when as a consequence of these attacks he offered to cancel an engagement to speak at a forthcoming Anglo-Catholic Congress in the Albert Hall, his offer was immediately accepted by the committee of the self-styled "Church Union," which had organized the congress. It is only fair to say that many of the most famous Anglo-Catholic priests—men like Father James Adderley and Father Jellicoe, dissociated themselves from the action of this committee and wrote to Dick to sympathize with him.

§

But his real quarrel with ecclesiasticism was that its noble professions of faith seemed so sadly at variance with its actual preoccupations and achievements. "I wonder," he wrote, "how we must appear to those who hear us making our brave assertions about the fatherhood of God, the brotherhood of man, and our personal devotion to the Lord Christ. I wonder if we do not seem to them like Alpine climbers who, having greased their faces and covered them with masks, and having put on their nailed boots and taken ice-axes in their hands, then proceed to walk gravely up the mild heights of Ludgate Hill? The contrast between our profession and our achievement would be ludicrous if it were not so utterly pathetic."

Dick felt that the leaders of the Church were far too cautious, lacking in adventurous courage, fearful of making mistakes, unduly sensitive to the opinions of the rich and titled members of the ecclesiastical assemblies, far too much concerned with the defence of the Church's status and traditions, and far too little with what is after all its main concern, the winning of the world to faith in Jesus Christ and all he stood for; a task which can never be fulfilled by those who are afraid to take great risks. "For many years now," he wrote in *If I were Dictator*, "I have come to feel that the Church is a frightened church. That is my main complaint. The Church has within it, I believe, the power of resurrection, but at the moment it is dying of pernicious anaemia. The Church is attempting to preserve itself without realizing that should it be willing to risk its life for the Gospel's sake, it might live again to the glory of God." He deplored, as many of us deplored, the contrast between the immense efforts made by the Church's leaders to prevent the passing of the Welsh Disestablishment Bill—the public meetings presided over and harangued by bishops and archbishops, the intensive propaganda in the press and by leaflets—and the comparative weakness and half-heartedness of efforts made from time to time in support of infinitely more important causes, such as the cause of peace.

Perhaps among the greatest of all his disappointments was the preoccupation of the Church Assembly with what seemed to him trivial domestic concerns at moments of world crisis. The truth is that the Church Assembly tends to be composed very largely, if not entirely, of blameless clergy and laity who have never really "adventured" in the course of their lives: men and women who have kept themselves in the public eye at purely ecclesiastical gatherings and have there gained a reputation for being 'safe' people: clergymen who can be trusted to defend the 'parson's freehold' and other purely this-world clerical interests; and ecclesiastical laymen who are even more conservative than the parsons themselves in their outlook. And the Assembly tends to be dominated by ecclesiastical lawyers—men of the type of Lord Quickswood, clever and fluent speakers, staunchly traditionalist, and quite out of touch with the great mass of ordinary lay folk. In the Assembly the 'important people,' in a strictly worldly sense, men with titles or wealth, are treated as though pre-eminence in the things of this world entitled them to pre-eminence in the Church, which only shows how different is the attitude of the Church Assembly from that of, say, St Paul.

All this was the more profoundly disappointing to Dick for the very reason that the Church Assembly was the only fruit which his great campaign for Life and Liberty seemed to have borne. He quotes, in one of his books, from a volume published by some of the chaplains in the first world-war under the title *The Church in the Furnace*—a book which he rightly describes as "filled with reforming zeal"—this passage:

> "We are a new race, we priests of France, humbled by much strain and much failure; revolutionaries not at all in spirit, but actually in fact, and while often enough we sigh for the former days, the procession of splendid offices, and the swell of the organ, these will never content us again, unless or until the great multitude also find their approach to God through them."

And this is Dick's own comment on the passage: "Was that only war-strain and shell-shock? Or had they then a vision which has strangely departed?"

> "Anyhow, overseas and at home, we were restless and dissatisfied then, and we said it. Now, though we ought to be equally dissatisfied since nothing worth

while came out of that discontent, we do not bemoan any longer. It is not done. We have gone back to 'the procession of splendid officers and the swell of the organ,' but I see no sign that the great multitude is any nearer 'finding their approach to God through them' than it was."

"In God's name," Dick cries, "has our generation not been blooded spiritually and physically enough for the last twenty years to learn the worth-while things? Am I disloyal in crying aloud to church people? Am I not perhaps right in my contention that a prophet is needed to wake us from our lethargy and our stupor, or must the following from the agenda of the Church Assembly be typical of our ecclesiastical reforming?

"'It is possible that separate sittings of the House of Clergy and the House of Laity may be arranged to consider the Banns of Matrimony Measure. In connection with this measure the report will be presented of the Commission appointed in June 1932 to examine the question of the publication of Banns of Marriage, with special reference to the publication of Banns by lay readers, and to consider the question of residence for the publication of Banns. There are main and majority reports on the subject.'

"That is from the *Church Times* of May 1934, under the headline Summer Task of the Church Assembly. Is not impatience justified? The late Lord Oxford and Asquith once remarked about the proceedings of a certain society that when he read its agenda in all its pompous array he was reminded of itinerant vendors of vegetable matter perambulating the streets of Baghdad with their loud cries of 'In the name of Allah! Figs!' That is an exact comment on the attitude of the bishops and leading churchmen who are content at this present time to cry 'Banns' in the hearing of the people. As well, or better, cry 'Bananas.' If this matter of banns must be attended to . . . by all means let it be done behind the scenes and without any further delay. It is small wonder that the Disarmament Conference was attended with such disaster if during the same month the Church Assembly, which should be guiding our people in making right judgements, could have the heart to advertise so trifling a matter as banns in the forefront of its agenda. What can be expected from a body bereft of all sense of imagination, proportion and humour? Truly the Church remains 'fierce when Christ was gentle and complacent when he was terrifying' while we suffer this grotesque assemblage in silence" (*Dictator*, pp. 22 ff.).

The reforms for which Dick pleaded in regard to St Paul's cathedral will hardly seem 'revolutionary' to anyone but the most hardened worshipper of tradition. To illuminate the cross on the dome; to keep the cathedral open until 7 p.m.: to have a canon or minor canon always available at luncheon hour for anyone needing spiritual help; to substitute for elaborately sung daily offices, which no one attends, beautiful and dignified services of not more than thirty-five minutes' duration, at say, 12 and 6 o'clock; to take steps to make it known that the chapter desired the great cathedral to become of greater service to the toiling masses who pass it by day by day—common sense would surely welcome such proposals, if it had any common love behind it.

The late Canon Deane in his autobiography, *Time Remembered*, writes of Dick, in this connection, "He was utterly certain that the schemes he propounded were right, that their adoption would be for the good of St Paul's and the Church; he simply could not understand the weighty objections to them which were evident to his colleagues"—but he does not give a hint of what those "weighty objections" were and the sad fact remains that Dick, before ever he came to St Paul's, had proved at Canterbury that he knew—as certainly none of his colleagues in the chapter who opposed him knew—how to make a great cathedral a real 'House of prayer for all people.' But, among other evidences of a lack of proportion in Mr Roberts's life of Dick, I think it must be admitted, in all fairness to Dick's fellow members of the chapter of St Paul's cathedral, that he grossly exaggerates their opposition to Dick's proposals. Many of those proposals were actually accepted and put into practice by the chapter.

It is worth recording here how in one particular instance Dick combined the wisdom of the serpent with the harmlessness of a dove in his dealings with the chapter. He proposed that a great Christmas-tree should be erected outside St Paul's, as had been done years before at St Martin's, and when he was assured that some of the chapter would oppose any such innovation, he managed to convey a suggestion to the King himself that he should offer to supply a Christmas-tree for this purpose. King George was delighted by the suggestion, and however ready any member of the chapter might be to oppose a suggestion made by Dick, they could hardly do other than welcome it when it came from no less a person than the Sovereign himself. I remember Dick's chuckle as he told me this.

5

Editor, Journalist, Broadcaster

IT would not be true to say that Dick revolutionized ecclesiastical journalism—would to God he had!

Apart from the more or less weighty theological reviews, ecclesiastical journals fall broadly speaking into quite definite classes. First there are the weekly organs, some of which represent one or other of the parties in the Church. The *Church Times*, Anglo-Catholic, ably edited and, as Dick would have agreed, more conspicuously "Catholic" than Christian, has long and deservedly had a high reputation among ecclesiastical journals as a medium for advertisements. It used to have a large circulation among kitchen-maids looking for jobs and mistresses looking for kitchen-maids. The most well-known among its recent editors, Mr Sydney Dark, astonished some of his Anglo-Catholic friends by proclaiming that Dick Sheppard was a saint. At the other ecclesiastical extreme there was *The Record*, the organ of a pious, orthodox and narrow Evangelicism. Between the two came *The Guardian*, respectable, orthodox, safe and sometimes, it must be admitted, ponderously dull. Early in this century there appeared for all too short a period an admirable journal, *The Pilot*, edited by the late Mr Lathbury. That is survived for so brief a time is sad testimony to the intelligence of the clergy and ecclesiastical laity. Just before the first world war there was launched a weekly paper called *The Challenge*. It was sponsored by a brilliant group of young men and was edited for a time by William Temple, afterwards archbishop of Canterbury. *The Challenge* died after a somewhat chequered career, largely because it was impossible in war-time to get sufficient of those advertisements which are the financial life-blood of any weekly journal; but still more because the ablest of those who would have been its most distinguished contributors gave their lives in the war, or were too busily engaged in it to have time for writing.

But below the stratum of these recognized journals there exist innumerable parish magazines, edited by their incumbents, usually incorporating an inset published by some firm interested in such matters, and for the most part filled with a mixture of pious sentimental articles and serial stories written by ecclesiastically-minded lay women, and a queer assortment of quasi-religious cross-word and other puzzles, competitions and what not. The chief feature of the parish magazine proper is the vicar's monthly letter—extracts from which, quite unconsciously humorous, from time to time add to the gaiety of *Punch's* Charivaria.

§

Dick was utterly disgusted by the poor standard of most of this ecclesiastical stuff, the unprincipled party spirit manifested by some of them, and the appalling triviality of the average parish magazine. And soon after he became vicar of St Martin's he decided to make what proved to be one of his most successful ventures: to publish a parish magazine of quite a new kind. The true function of a parish magazine, he argued, is to give its readers a truly catholic outlook: to help them to realize what men are thinking and doing in the world of everyday life: and to take if possible the truly Christian view of all the various problems and crises which loom so large in the secular press and are the concern of the true follower of Jesus Christ, even more than of the famous stoic who first wrote that nothing human was outside his interest. So *St Martin's Review* was to welcome contributions from thinkers of all kinds who had something they felt it important to say, whether they belonged to this or that ecclesiastical party, whether they called themselves Christian or not. Humour was not to be excluded, for a sense of humour goes with the power to see things in their right proportions. There was a section devoted to reviews of all the most important books, including novels, that were published. And there were notices of plays and other forms of public entertainment. All purely parochial concerns, such as the activities of St Martin's Fellowship, notices of forthcoming events and so forth, were relegated to a few pages at the ends of each number, under the heading "Matters merely Parochial."

§

The Review was from the first an amazing success. Bertine Buxton has told how at the outset the then senior curate of St Martin's sportingly bet Dick a fiver that he would never sell a thousand copies. Six years later its circulation had reached 10,000 copies a month and a special double number "one glorious single month had rocketed up to a sale of 23,000 copies." Dick was, in fact, among so many other things, a born editor, and with his usual acumen he found an ideal sub-editor and manager in Bertine Buxton (Mrs. Ewan Hay), who loved the Review as much as he did. I am indebted to her for this account of Dick as editor.

> "Dick had a genius for knowing what public feeling was before it had crystallized into public expression. He kept his finger, as it were, on the pulse of ordinary men and women. One of the best examples of this was the way Armistice day was degenerating into festivities only, without remembrance or thanksgiving, and thereby causing much pain to those who had lost people in the war. Many will remember how he took over the Albert Hall from those who had arranged a

huge charity ball on November 11th, guaranteeing a sum of money to them, and instead organized a service of remembrance. By an editorial in *St Martin's Review* and a letter to *The Times*, he altered, and saved, the whole character of the day for that year and all future years.

"When he deemed that a thing needed saying, or a topic airing, he did not mind how unpopular it was, or how much criticism or abuse it brought down on his paper. If people cancelled their subscriptions as a result of some strong article he was delighted, as he felt it had got home; and he always said, 'For everyone who cancels we shall get two new readers.' He had no thought of playing for safety, and indeed in one instance he was definitely disappointed when a large paper did not bring a libel action which he had expected to follow some outspoken criticism.

"As long as *St Martin's Review* was his own paper and his name appeared on it as sole editor he was fearless of all criticism and results, said all that he felt needed saying, and gloried in being provocative. But the moment he had a co-editor (Pat McCormick) all this fire and zest was quenched, for he was over-careful not to involve anyone else in any difficulty or controversy.

"Personally I think all his work showed him to be a man to work on his own, following his own instinct, rather than reasoning things out. When he worked with organizations his work lost so much, because he was over-sensitive to the feelings of his colleagues and in his efforts to spare them he lost his spontaneity.

"He was never, in my opinion, as effective as he had been at St Martin's, either at Canterbury or St Paul's, where he had to work as a member of a chapter, or even at the P.P.U., where he worked with a committee. Working with him after Pat became nominally co-editor was really a heart-breaking experience for me. All his fire went. He adored the Review and had been sorely tempted to take it away with him from St Martin's and run it as an independent Christian monthly. I confess that I longed for him to do so, and I still think that the Review would have served a wonderful purpose and had a huge sale. But on reflection Dick felt that to do this would not be fair to Pat.

"I used to go and meet him in all sorts of odd places to discuss the Review, when it was at its zenith: at railway stations, dentists' waiting-rooms, nursing homes. Suddenly there would come a telephone message to go to him; and there he was, bursting with ideas that had come to him during the hours of a sleepless night. Often, too, we would have a meeting on the Review, perhaps Dick, Hugo [the Rev. Hugh Johnston], Ewan and myself, or just a meeting between him and myself. I would leave him at about 7 or 8 p.m. Next morning there would be a letter from him—posted outside the vicarage at midnight—elaborating a plan or producing a quite new one. He was just a gloriously vital person to work with in those days. 'Put on your best hat, Bertine, and go along to the House and see what old Lansbury is thinking,' he would say—or it might be Father Groser in the East End, or Harold Craxton at the Coliseum, or St John Ervine or Forbes Robertson, the actor, or Inge or Galsworthy or just anybody.

"Now [concludes Bertine, sadly] as one looks round, his work as such does not seem to be alive anywhere. I don't think many of the customs or clubs etc. which he started still go on. But *he* goes on in hundreds and hundreds of ordinary men and women's hearts, having quite changed their outlook and still continuing, year after year, to be their 'yardstick.'"

§

"However eminent may be the theologians, however eloquent the preachers, however finished the services from cathedrals and churches throughout the country, it was in large measure the vision, the courage, the eager personality and the passionate sincerity of H. R. L. Sheppard which gave religion its established place in the broadcasting service. *Vivit enim, vivetque semper.*" So wrote Sir J. C. W. Reith (now Lord Reith) soon after Dick Sheppard's death. And he revealed then that the idea of broadcasting a complete religious service from a church was first broached, on 14th June 1923, at a lunch at Simpson's with Dick.

It was on the first Sunday of the following year that the first of the famous broadcast services from St Martin-in-the-Fields took place. I suppose few realize now the immense courage it required on Dick's part to make this great experiment. To many people the very idea of a broadcast service seemed sacrilegious, almost blasphemous. Many of the clergy feared that if services were broadcast, to which people could listen at their own fire-sides, their already dwindling congregations would diminish even more rapidly. But to Dick it seemed that the invention of broadcasting was in fact a new God-given opportunity to bring the inspiration and comfort of religion to thousands who hitherto had had little chance of knowing what faith in Jesus Christ really meant. So he threw himself with all his passionate zeal into 'the buying-up' of this new opportunity of service.

There can be no doubt that the immense new strain which broadcasting threw upon his already overtaxed strength helped to undermine his health and to shorten his life. It was not only that he put into his actual services and sermons everything that he had to give—and how much that was!—but, as I have already noted, his broadcast addresses involved him in a new and vast correspondence with those countless people who wrote not merely to thank him for help he had given them by his words, but to seek the advice of one whose sincerity, sympathy and understanding of human nature and human need was so unmistakable. Whole nights Dick would sit up writing, writing, writing. . . . He would never leave a letter unanswered and to those whose need seemed to be greatest and most personal he always wrote in his own hand. And after such a night at his desk he would have a bath, go off to celebrate Holy Communion at St Martin's, and so to breakfast and yet another day of ceaseless work. No wonder his health broke down under the strain: no wonder he was attacked by insomnia as well as asthma. I remember remonstrating with him about this habit of night-long writing between days of incredible strain. It was quite in vain. All he would reply was "Charlie, I must do the job in the only way in which I can do it at all."

What was it that made Dick Sheppard the incomparable religious broadcaster that he undoubtedly was? The answer is not far to seek. He had to a unique extent the gift of being able to get across to his listeners that love which burned in his heart for all sad, troubled, perplexed and burdened men and women. That love was never more apparent than when he himself was suffering in mind and body, as he so often was when he laboured with too little breath up the steps of St Martin's pulpit. Though he never obtruded himself in any way, he was in fact the man, described by the psalmist as blessed, who "going through the vale of misery uses it for a well"; and the water of that well was indeed, for countless numbers of those who listened so eagerly to him, the water of life.

I can only remember hearing two criticisms of Dick's broadcast preaching. The first was the comparatively trivial one of what seemed to the critic a meaningless mannerism—the upward inflection of his voice at the end of his sentences, which did indeed become a meaningless mannerism in some of those preachers who foolishly tried to imitate him. But in Dick that habit arose, I believe, in the main, from the attempt to overcome the breathlessness caused by his asthma; though possibly it was due in some measure to his determination to avoid the opposite mannerism, so prevalent among preachers, of so dropping the voice at the end of each sentence as to become almost inaudible.

The second, and more serious criticism, was to the effect that his preaching showed no profundity or originality of thought. With that criticism Dick himself, who was the humblest of men, would have whole-heartedly agreed. He never professed to be a profound thinker, and in the commonly accepted sense of those words he was right. Mr Middleton Murry justly says of him, "Dick's humility was absolute. 'I've no brains, Middleton,' he would say, and he meant it. Yet the truth was he had a rare and subtle intelligence. He was far wiser than most men dreamed."

But I should like to ask those critics who so judged Dick's preaching exactly what they mean by 'originality' and 'profundity.' 'Originality' in a thinker may mean that he has thought what no one else has ever thought before him, and in that sense Dick was not an original thinker. 'Profundity' may mean that the thinker has attained to a deeper understanding of ultimate reality than other thinkers have reached. In that sense Dick was not perhaps a profound thinker. But if originality in a thinker means, as it may, that the thoughts he expresses are his own real thoughts—not so to speak secondhand thoughts, snatched (as many preachers thoughts are) from some one else's writing, with no genuine personal experience of the preacher's behind them, then Dick's preaching was most certainly 'original.' And if 'profundity' means, as it may mean, that a man's thoughts are the fruit of his personal contact with ultimate reality, then again Dick's thought was very often truly profound.

For the power and value of Dick's preaching came, when all is said, from the fact that he prayed ceaselessly for the Holy Spirit—the Spirit of Love, which is truth; and truth which is love. And that his constant prayer for the Spirit was abundantly answered is manifested in the simple fact that, like the Master he served, he 'knew'—as too few preachers seem to know—'what was in man,' and so was able, as too few preachers are able, to bring help to untold thousands of his fellow men. I think that it is true to say that no other Anglican preacher in my day, with the possible exception of Father Stanton, could more certainly stir the hearts and wills of those who heard him.

If Dick never succeeded in bringing about the revolution he longed to see in the official church; if his campaign to convert the world to pacifism was doomed to fail; at least he revolutionized the lives of more individuals than any other preacher of his day, giving new hope to the hopeless, new strength to the weak, new courage to the fearful and above all love to the loveless and unloved.

In my own mind I am certain that no other of the preachers who have broadcast since his day has ever had so wide a response as that which Dick awoke in the hearts of literally millions of listeners. To that fact the immense concourse of people of all ranks and classes who filed past his coffin as he lay in his beloved St Martin's church after his death, and lined the streets and thronged St Paul's Cathedral to the doors on the day of his funeral, bore unmistakable witness.

6

"The Human Parson" and his Axiom

BY far the best of Dick Sheppard's books, in my estimation, is the little volume which bears the title put in inverted commas at the head of this chapter. It represents the substance of a course of lectures on pastoral theology delivered at Cambridge in 1923—when Dick was at the height of his powers at St Martin-in-the-Fields. It has been many times reprinted; and it is certainly a book which every young man who is hoping to be ordained would do well to read and ponder over. It reveals, as no other of his books reveals, Dick's own ideal of what a parson should be. And to those who knew and admired him it is also a reminder of how faithfully he himself followed the path he pointed out to others.

In this little book too there shines out his great love for the Church, and in particular for that branch of it to which he belonged, the Church of England; and his ideal of what that church might accomplish if all its officials and ministers, especially in their assemblies, would only continually lay themselves open to what in another of his books he calls "the wind of the Spirit." I have already quoted from this book one long passage. Here is another characteristic passage, from his opening lecture:

> "One does not have to be despondent about the future of the Christian religion to realize that there is a very real reconstruction taking place in the minds of many thoughtful people—this is not limited to the young. They have a large conception of the things Jesus Christ cared about and came to teach. He is as real to them—perhaps more so than He ever was—but they are less

anxious to define Him. I should be inclined to say that He has become so real, so great, and so many-sided that they feel, however great the necessity, the total inadequacy of attempting to say in a document, long or short, just what He is, for man has no celestial language. They are glad to retain the capital H and to leave their definition at that. They fear that the official demand for any definition, which must be partial, will tend to deny such light as is breaking in on men who see Him from other sides.

"The conception of the Jesus of history as being so much larger than His church is making many a thoughtful parson and layman profoundly uninterested in some of the questions which seem of fundamental importance to the ecclesiastically-minded. It is possible to love one's church passionately, and perhaps with equal passion believe in it, not perhaps exactly as it is but as it might be, and yet to feel that a great deal of its energy is at the moment being spent on work to which its Founder would attach little, if any importance, and on the emphasizing of matters which He might totally and even indignantly disregard."

And here is yet another passage, which reveals Dick's whole position in regard to the Church and church reform:

"For myself I am prouder of nothing than that I am permitted to be a humble official of a Society that might save the soul of the world and bring endless joy to the hearts of mankind.

"I know that official actions of clergy who think as I do appear from time to time as disloyal to the letter of the Church's law, while others find it hard to understand how, holding the views we do, we are still content to use official forms which we earnestly desire altered and perform official ceremonies which have very little but good intention to be said for them. For myself I can only say that wherever possible, in and sometimes out of season, I urge the most radical reform of many of the Church's ceremonies and formularies, and beyond that I dare to believe that my Master will understand and pardon what seems to be insincere if He knows that the real purpose of my ministry be to make Him known and loved of men, and to do what I humbly can from within His Society to make it more worthy of His presence."

The simple truth is that for Dick the whole of the Christian religion consisted in complete loyalty to Jesus as he saw Him in the gospels and as he had found Him in his own religious experience. He really did believe what all Christians say that they believe—that God was incarnate in the very man Jesus; that as St Paul says, "God was in Christ, reconciling the world to himself" (2 Cor. ix. 19) And he saw that for this very reason it is impossible for anyone to know 'divinity,' or become in very deed a 'divine,' unless he is fully and completely human.

He believed, with that great philosopher A. S. Pringle-Pattison, that men "are apt to limit and mechanize the great doctrine of the Incarnation, which forms the centre of the Christian faith. . . . 'God manifest in the flesh' is a more profound philosophical truth than the loftiest flight of speculation that outsoars all predicates and, for the greater glory of God, declares Him unknowable" (*The Idea of God in Recent Philosophy*, p. 157). Too many parsons are in fact what they seem to their people to be: somehow less than human, without being at all divine. It was the secret of Dick's power that he was always so utterly human that God could manifest Himself through him to those who sought Him.

It was for this reason that Dr. L. P. Jacks could write of him:

> "Dick Sheppard was (and still is) a living proof of the existence of God. Were all other proofs to fail us, a life and character such as his—and he was one of a great apostolic succession—would be enough to justify us in saying that God is, and that God is Love. There was in him that spirit of devoted love for his fellow men, which is the life and driving force of true religion whatsoever form it may take, and can only be accounted for as the action, in the human field, of the force which creates, sustains and animates the entire universe. I met him only once—though we corresponded—and my thought as I left him was something like this. 'Were all other proofs to fail me, that man alone would compel me to believe that God exists and that God is Love.' In none whom I have known in these days has the light of the Spirit shone with a brighter or a steadier flame. And now it has gone out, but only to burn elsewhere and not, thank God, till many another candle had been kindled at its flame. I think the hour of his departure was appointed him. But his work will last.
>
> > "*It will last, and shine transfigured*
> > *In the final reign of Right;*
> > *It will pass into the splendours*
> > *Of the City of the Light.*"

Never surely was a greater or a juster tribute paid by a supreme thinker to a man who only thought of himself as a humble parson.

But if Dick was himself a gloriously human parson, he never made the quite fatal mistake made by some young parsons in their anxiety to get into touch with men—made, as more than one man in the forces has assured me, by some of the chaplains in the late war—of trying to get into touch with men by showing that you are not afraid to curse when they curse and drink when they drink. Men want to see in their parson not a poor copy of themselves at their worst, but a man who, in his life as well as in his words, while he mixes freely with them, shows them how they may become what they feel in their heart of hearts they ought to be, and want, in their better moments at all events, to become. For they know well enough, what Professor Jacks is so fond of pointing out, that there is a hero and a coward in every man. They know that they have in themselves a capacity for high and ennobling self-sacrifice in a great cause, even while they are weak enough to condone their own self-indulgences. And such ordinary men saw in Dick a man—as true a man as ever lived—in whom somehow the hero had triumphed over the coward; a man who, through the grace of God, had cast out self-indulgence by the power of a living faith; a man whom they could love whole-heartedly, because he so obviously loved them.

So Dick's passionate plea for humanity in the parson was no plea that he should exhibit an unredeemed humanity, for the humanity he worshipped and preached, yes, and lived as few have lived it, was the humanity he saw in Jesus Christ.

§

"It has become a commonplace to say nowadays," writes D. R. Davies in another book in this series (*Reinhold Niebuhr*, p. 58) "that there can be no revolution without a theory." What then, it may be asked, was the theory in Dick Sheppard's mind and expressed in his books? The answer is not far to seek. Dick's theory was in fact a very simple one, so simple, indeed, that he treated it as an axiom, the self-evident truth of which everyone must surely acknowledge. It was simply this that "A church may not be corporately less Christian than the individual Christian."

I do not think he ever thought out theoretical objections to this idea. He was never primarily a thinker for thought's sake, as so many theologians seem to be. His interest always lay in action. Be that as it may, this was the criterion by which he judged all the activities of the official Church: judged them and found them sadly wanting. He looked out on organized religion in all its manifestations, and in particular on the Church of England as it expressed its corporate mind in the manifestoes of the bishops at their conferences, and the activities of Convocation and the Church Assembly, and nowhere did the mind of the Church seem to accord, as he believed it ought to accord, with the mind of the Church's Founder as he saw that mind mirrored in the pages of the gospels. So he pleaded for a new conversion in the Church.

> "My contention is," he wrote, "that the task now awaiting every Church . . . is to put itself corporately and ruthlessly under the tuition of Jesus Christ in an atmosphere of unlimited candour, that it may correct its values where they have gone astray, simplify its message where it has become immensely complicated, purify its life and witness where it has suffered from contact with the kingdoms of this world, and dissociate itself from the spirit of exclusiveness and from privileges which separate it from other churches, and render it incomprehensible to and aloof from ordinary people who have nothing but admiration for the religion of Christ as they find it in His life. This will be no light undertaking. The sharing of the mind of Christ will be almost as difficult as rebirth itself for churches rooted in history and sometimes in those fables that are called history (I am not afraid of history but I *am* afraid of historians!)—steeped in tradition, jealous of prestige, tenacious of their status, confident in the finality of their creeds, anxious for pre-eminence. 'To covet the truth

is a very distinguished passion,' says Santayana. A world of vested interests is not one which welcomes the disruptive forces of candour, but unless the churches will consent at least to reconsider their values, judgements and traditions under a new baptism of the Spirit of Jesus Christ, Christendom cannot be renewed; if they will, then surprising things will happen, the result of which no man can foretell."

In regard to "those fables that are called history," Dick in a footnote remarks, "there is a wealth of truth in Mark Twain's delightful saying, 'I had a splendid education, but the worst of it is that so much of it wasn't so' " (*Impatience*, pp. 33 f.). Dick's pleas for reform in the Church were based in reality upon one profound truth, better expressed perhaps by A. C. Turner, a brilliant young Fellow of Trinity College, Cambridge, who was killed in the first world-war, than by anyone else. Turner wrote very searchingly on the relation of the Church to its Founder. After pointing out that all spiritual progress comes in the first instance through Spirit-possessed individuals, he says:

"Nor is the individual ever exhausted in that part of him which becomes the property of his successors. The prophet attracts a school, and through it his work is continued and becomes in part incorporate in the beliefs and practices of men. But there is something in the individual to which men return when the '-ism' which is called by his name grows cold and inadequate. It was necessary that he should become institutionalized, as it was necessary that Christ should become the foundation of that mass of custom and doctrine which men identify with the Church. But the founder is always more than the institution and than the theory which is built upon his work. To that 'More' men must ever return—to the intellectual faith of Plato from the diverse opinions which pass as Platonism, to the life and person of Christ from the warring organizations which compete for His name. Through organizations and generalities his work flows back into the general body of social life. But it is never exhausted in this; it finds its fulfilment in the individual inspiration and endeavour of His spiritual children, through whom it begets ever richer values in relation to changed circumstances and fuller knowledge. Always the individual is more than the general and through the individual the Spirit enters more fully into its heritage" (*Concerning Prayer*, p. 402).

Dick was one of those spirit-possessed individuals who judged the Church of his day by going back to that "More" in the Church's Founder of which Turner writes.

He was indeed really up against the everlasting paradox that a church, an organization, is absolutely necessary to Christianity, or indeed to any religion, if it is to survive and be spread abroad; but that no church has ever been, or could conceivably be, run by men who were on the same spiritual level as its Founder. Dick himself, with all his faults, was Christlike in one thing. He was possessed by an infinite love and compassion for the great multitude of ordinary men and women, who seemed to him, as they had seemed to his Master, to be "distressed and scattered abroad as sheep not having a shepherd": and not merely distressed and scattered, but led by "blind leaders of the blind" to the needless slaughter of war. And the official Church, he felt, which ought to be possessed and driven by a Christlike love and compassion, seemed to be far more deeply concerned about its own status, its own trivial domestic concerns, than about the fate of the men and women it was commissioned to save. While Rome was burning, the official Church was content to look on and fiddle.

§

Dick's plea is really the old plea, so often uttered, so rarely acted upon—to 'put first things first.' And Dick felt that the bishops themselves did not realize what were 'the first things'; or, if they did, were content to allow them to be put, in practice, far behind mere trivialities. I remember his saying to me once about a friend of his, now a bishop, "Dear old X spends all his time running about from conference to conference—always arriving late from his last conference, and leaving early to arrive (still late) at his next; always saying, 'We must put first things first,' and saying it at considerable length, but never letting us know—does he know himself?—what those 'first things' really are."

Dick was sure—and rightly sure—that he knew what those 'first things' were which must be put first, if the world was to be saved from irreparable disaster. Love, Christlike in its self-sacrifice and self-giving, that is the thing which must always be 'put first': love for the God revealed as love in Jesus Christ; love for the great multitude of those who were being blindly led into the great abyss. The official Church he felt, instead of standing as Jesus stood, for God's way of life in stark opposition to the way of the greedy, selfish, mammon-worshipping world, was itself infiltrated by the very spirit of that world. Was he wrong in all this? I wish I could believe that he was.

"I do not believe," he cried, "that there is any worthwhile future for a Christian church that will not here and now suffer the fresh air of its Lord's simplicity to sweep through those dusty assemblies, conferences, and parochial meetings, where men sit postponing all ethical discussions or making futile pronouncements upon them, and arguing over matters that are sometimes alien to Christianity and sometimes even alien to religion" (*If I were Dictator*, p. 31).

And he noticed sadly, what many others have noticed,

that 'the best and most thoughtful men and women' were 'leaving the Church not because of what is worst in them, but because of what is best. They do not believe that churches so obviously playing for safety, so complicated with irrelevant values and subtleties, so ensnared in that evil—beloved of nations—as to which and who shall be the greatest, can be God's last word for these great days, or provide authentic information about the spiritual world' (*Ibid.*, p. 31).

Churches 'playing for safety,' their leaders obviously afraid lest they should be accused by their more fanatical followers of having given away their partisan position, priding themselves, even as they descended from platforms on which they had made eloquent harangues in the cause of reunion, on having 'given nothing away'—that it was which made Dick so rightly impatient. How could Christians lead the world into the paths of unity and peace, if they could not find unity and peace among themselves; if they were unwilling to make *real* sacrifices themselves, in that great cause? Churches, no less than individuals, were under the inexorable law, 'Whosoever would save his life shall lose it.'

Dick discriminated, as too few discriminate, between that uniformity which smaller men make their aim and that all-embracing unity which allows for and welcomes within itself an infinite diversity of order and means of expression, which is surely the more Christlike ideal. Dick's own position in regard to unity, as against uniformity, was strongly reinforced by the conclusions arrived at by that great scholar, B. H. Streeter, and published in his well-known book *The Primitive Church*. Streeter wrote:

> "For four hundred years theologians of rival churches have armed themselves to battle on the question of the Primitive Church. However great their reverence for

scientific truth and historic fact, they have at least *hoped* that the result of their investigations would be to vindicate apostolic authority for the type of Church Order to which they themselves were attached. The Episcopalian has sought to find episcopacy, the Presbyterian presbyterianism, and the Independent a system of independency, to be the form of church government in New Testament times. But while each party to the dispute has been able to make out a case for his own view, he has never succeeded in demolishing the case of his opponent. The explanation of this deadlock, I have come to believe, is quite simple. It is the uncriticized assumption, made by all parties to the controversy, that in the first century there existed a single type of Church Order.

"Approach the evidence without making that assumption and two conclusions come into sight: (1) In the New Testament itself there can be traced an evolution of Church Order, comparable to the development in theological reflection detected by the scholarship of the last century. (2) The most natural interpretation of the evidence is that, at the end of the first century A.D., there existed, in different provinces of the Roman Empire, different systems of church government. Among these the Episcopalian, the Presbyterian, and the Independent can each discover the prototype of the system to which he himself adheres.

"The hypothesis of a primitive diversity in Christian institutions may, or may not, succeed in commending itself to the judgement of scholars; but in the mean time it has, at any rate, one merit: it is not likely to add fuel to the flames of ecclesiastical controversy. Indeed if my hypothesis is correct, then, in the classic words of *Alice in Wonderland*, 'Everyone has won, and all shall have prizes.' At any rate, I am entitled to assume that—

among those who profess and call themselves Christians —there will be but few of those unfortunates, to whom it is no satisfaction to be right unless they can thereby put others in the wrong."

But if Streeter was right in his contention that in the earliest days of the Church there was unity but not uniformity, then Dick in his refusal to listen to the demands of the rigid 'uniformitarians'—if one may coin a word as ugly as the theory it enshrines is deplorable—was, as indeed the Dean of St Paul's said in his moving address in St Paul's Cathedral at Dick's funeral service, 'a primitive Christian in the modern world.' And no doubt the dean was right when he added that such a primitive Christian "must be to some degree an alien and a rebel." Would there were more such aliens and rebels among the clergy of the Church to-day!

7

Warring World and Divided Church

IT was in 1936 that Dick founded the Peace Pledge Union. Two years earlier he had sent his famous letter to the press inviting those who agreed with him to send him a postcard saying that they renounced war and would never again, directly or indirectly, support or sanction another. It was the overwhelming response which came to this letter which led him to found the P.P.U.

In actual fact the members of the P.P.U. were an oddly assorted crew. Dick was a pacifist for two reasons. First, he had been absolutely tortured by the suffering he had witnessed in the hospital to which he acted as chaplain in France in the early days of the 1914 war, and by the discovery of the fact that war, so far from ennobling men, too often ruins them not merely in body but in soul. He discovered, as he himself wrote at the time, that war was "more awful than I supposed possible." But he became a pacifist, also, because he became convinced that war was utterly contrary to the mind of Jesus Christ, and that therefore those who framed the thirty-seventh Article were wrong in maintaining that 'It is lawful for Christian men, at the commandment of the Magistrate, to wear weapons, and serve in the wars.'

Was he wrong or right in this conviction? I felt at the time when he embarked on his Pleace Pedge campaign that he was wrong, though I disagreed, as strongly as he did, with some of the pleas put forward in opposition to pacifism by Archbishop Temple and others. But men become 'pacifists' for many different reasons, many of them far less convincing than Dick's. Nobody wants war, except possibly armament-manufacturers and those few romantic die-hards who still cling obstinately to the belief that war—even mechanized war—is a noble and ennobling affair.

When war breaks out patriots of the 'Colonel Blimp' variety invariably lump all pacifists together as cranks and cowards. But the number of those who become pacifists from pure cowardice is, I am convinced, infinitesimal. In actual fact, in face of the feverish mass-patriotism aroused as a direct result of propaganda whenever war breaks out, and the appeal of such slogans as 'The Country is in Danger!' or (as in 1914), 'Your King and Country Need You,' it requires far more courage in a man of military age to resist the mass-emotion and accept the stigma of pacifism, than to join the armed forces. I was myself pilloried by Horatio Bottomley in *John Bull* for saying this in 1914.

But men may be pacifists from quite unchristian motives. They may have no nobler motive than their unwillingness to have their routine existence upset. They may even wish to show how superior they are to the masses of their fellow men. And there are, I fear, vast numbers who, while they are ready to cry "Peace, at any price," are yet quite unprepared to pay that price which must be paid if the reign of peace is ever to be established on earth.

Where I could never agree with Dick's P.P.U. policy—though, as I have said already, I just hated having to differ from him in anything, even though our difference never in any way affected our personal friendship—was that I felt that in getting all sorts of people, with all sorts of motives, to say that they would "renounce war, and never support or sanction another," was in effect to put the cart before the horse; and that the gain of having a comparatively simple objective, which people who were very far from being agreed on moral or religious grounds could accept, was altogether out-weighed by the simple fact that peace will always be impossible unless people are agreed *first* to seek "the things which belong to their peace."

How many centuries have passed since the prophet proclaimed the truth that it is 'justice' which 'brings peace,' and 'honesty' which 'renders men secure'! (Isaiah xxxii. 17; Moffatt's translation) Though it is almost impossible, I believe, to exaggerate the evil of war, I believe also that war itself is a symptom of a still deeper evil, and that until men combine to attack that deeper evil, it is useless to accept their pledges to renounce war.

Dick himself and many of his closest friends and followers were indeed prepared to 'seek first the kingdom of God and His righteousness' and so to pay the price of peace; but numbers signed his pledge who were by no means so prepared, and that, in my view, made the apparent success of his campaign altogether illusive. When I spoke to Dick about this he would only answer, "Yes; I think I see your point; and sometimes I feel exactly as you do." And then he would add, "But I must go on my own way. I can no other." So he went on; and his way, outwardly and as the world judges, was a triumphant way. Everywhere he went, up and down the country, people flocked to his meetings and applauded his speeches rapturously, and in ever-increasing numbers signed the famous pledge.

§

I ask myself now, after the war into which he so clearly foresaw that the world was drifting, what in the end was the result of all his toil? I remember one of the ablest bishops on the bench, some time after the latest war had started, shaking his head over Dick and his P.P.U. The movement, he said, had done untold harm: Hitler would never have risked war with this country if he had not believed that pacifism was so rampant here that no government in Great Britain would ever dare to go to war. But there is no evidence whatever, as far as I know, that Hitler would really have been restrained from the pursuit of his mad schemes of conquest, even by the complete certainty that the point would be reached when he would be involved in war with Great Britain and the Empire.

But I do think Dick was so possessed by the evil side of war, which indeed I have said it is impossible to exaggerate, that he was blind to what I dare to call, in spite of everything, the good side of it. "War," wrote Maxim Pavlovich Murov, "is the most outrageous thing. I am not thinking now of its horror and bestialities. I am thinking of its contradictions; of how, foul in itself, it brings forth the highest and noblest side of man's character, inspires man and raises him above himself, how for all its cruelty, it yet seems to fertilize the better passions" (*Red Surgeon,* by George Borodin). That I believe is true, paradoxical though it seems. It is perfectly true that war brutalizes men, ruins them, body and soul; and yet there are thousands who come back from war, not only not brutalized, not ruined, but actually finer and better men than they were before. And it is surely true that during both the great world wars this country was as a whole—despite all that may be urged to the contrary—animated by a nobler spirit than that which animated it during the dreadful years between 1918 and 1939, or alas! than animates it today.

Of course Dick was right in his conviction that war is utterly unchristian. Of course he was right in his realization that those who charged him with sentimentality were themselves far more open to that charge. The romantic view of war—especially of modern, mechanized war—is sentimentalist to the last degree. And Dick certainly exposed that sentimentalism in his books and speeches. Though I cannot agree with the opinion expressed by some critics, and endorsed even by the Dean of St Paul's, that *We Say "No,"* which has for a sub-title *The Plain Man's Guide to Pacifism,* is the best of all his books, I do think that in it he demolished once for all the favourite arguments of the militarists and exposed with devastating thoroughness their stupid sentimentalism. No one, however convinced he might be of the necessity of resorting to the arbitrament of war in some circumstances, could ever, after reading that book, use again the argument which was the stock-in-trade of the tribunals before which pacifists were hauled in the first world war, which ran, "Would you not fight to prevent your sister from being raped?" No open-minded man could feel after reading it that war was anything but a ghastly evil, at once the symptom and the cause of moral and religious decay. It is not impossible, of course, to criticize some of Dick's arguments. I think myself that he bases far too much on the command, "Thou shalt not kill." If that command is, as he argues, an 'unequivocal,' an 'absolute' command, it not only condemns war, but equally the taking of any form of life at all. It condemns most certainly capital punishment. It condemns—and Dick came to realize and accept this—every form of sport which involves killing; it condemns the shooting of a man-eating tiger, and fishing no less than hunting and shooting. It condemns all eating of meat, and even, logically—as G. K. Chesterton showed, in *The Napoleon of Notting Hill*—the eating of vegetables. But Dick, for all his insistence on the 'absoluteness' of this commandment, was himself illogical. He would not himself shoot, but he was quite ready to eat game shot by someone else. He was never a vegetarian. He never, as far as I know, protested against capital punishment. He, in fact, as Mr. Roberts shows, 'isolated war,' and by so doing both weakened and strengthened his case. He weakened it by laying himself open to the charge that he was dealing with a symptom and ignoring the real disease; or at least treating the symptom as though it was the whole evil. He strengthened it by restricting his campaign to one quite simple objective. He believed himself, and succeeded in persuading thousands of his fellow men to believe, that war is the greatest threat in the modern world to all true human progress and to any kind of Christian civilization.

For myself, I am absolutely convinced that he was, unhappily, right in his profound conviction that the official Church, and the vast majority of professing Christians, had betrayed Jesus Christ by refusing to accept the challenge of war and of the war-mongers to Christian ethics. After the first world war,

> "We gave thanks to God that there would be no more war, but we wanted peace without being willing to pay its price. It is our fault that the world trembles once more on the brink of the madness of blood. It is our fault—the fault of Christian men and women in all nations, but especially of Christian men, because we have been unwilling to accept the practical implications of our Christianity. Our faith has been a shadow, not a flame. We have worshipped God for an hour or so on Sunday, and tried to safeguard the rest of the week by means of a 'gentlemen's agreement' with the Devil. So we have won the peace that we deserve—a peace precariously poised upon the points of bayonets.
>
> "Peace cannot depend on armaments. It cannot be preserved by force. It cannot be organized, any more than love can be organized. We all know that in our hearts. But we have been afraid to act upon that knowledge. 'It is not our business. . . . We have given the politicians a mandate. . . . They know that we want peace, that another war would mean the end of civilization. It is their job, not ours, to see that peace is maintained, that war does not come again. And they also want peace. They have told us so, over and over again, in their speeches. Surely we can leave it to them.'
>
> "Well, we have left it to them. And they have given us

mechanized armies, squadrons of battle planes that darken the sun, bigger and better bombs, more lethal poison gas. God help the peace that rests on such foundations!

"But the fault is not the politicians'. It is our own. I believe that the great majority of the world's statesmen sincerely want peace. But they are still hypnotized by that Devil's paradox: 'If you want peace, prepare for war.' They believe in a peace of penalties—that if only war can be made sufficiently terrible, it will never happen. That a system of pacts and understandings, which make war automatic in certain eventualities, will prevent those eventualities arising. I can see their point of view. Their arguments are specious enough. And perhaps, for five, or ten, or twenty years, they will be able to slide from crisis to crisis, and still stave off the evil day. But it may come suddenly—like a thunder-blast.

"They know that. But so long as they place 'security' before peace; national interest, national prestige before peace, they can do no other. They are doing their duty according to their lights.

"I do not propose to attack the politicians. I give them every credit for sincerity. They are probably far wiser than I am. But the wisdom of this world is foolishness with God, and I am God's servant, pledged to obey His word. I believe that, at this time, a special responsibility rests upon all individual Christians and upon the Christian churches. I believe that the world is drifting towards war largely because we have not had the courage of our Christianity, and that, even at the eleventh hour, we may yet transform the situation if we forget all that we have been told about 'practical politics' and try instead a little practical religion" (*We Say "No,"* pp. 2 ff.).

§

I do not think that anyone who takes Christianity seriously can fail to agree with this indictment of the failure of the Church and the failure of individual Christians to accept the responsibility their faith imposes upon them to seek 'the things that belong to peace.' Where I differed from Dick was in the belief that war is not in itself the supreme evil, but only the most malignant symptom of that evil. I remember an essay written for me once by an able Marlborough boy on the true use of scientific knowledge. After demonstrating how science had increased man's power for good or evil, and dwelling on the prostitution of science to destructive ends in time of war, he went on to point out how science could be made to minister to man's real needs, and then ended his essay by saying that if scientific discovery were so used 'man would undoubtedly prosper and wax fat.' This is precisely the end which some pacifists seem to envisage, and it is precisely for this reason that so many militarists oppose pacifism. It seems to them to cut the heroic out of life. Are we here they ask for nothing better than to have material prosperity and "wax fat"?

Unless we recognize that there is a great ideal to be striven for beyond the elimination of war as a means of settling human disputes, we shall never arouse that passionate enthusiasm without which no great achievement is possible, enthusiasm comparable with that aroused by war itself, when men are persuaded that they are fighting for freedom. No doubt many different motives actuated those who hastened to join up in the first world war, and though conscription meant fewer actual volunteers for the fighting services in the second, yet thousands of men and women hastened to get trained for dangerous and exacting tasks in the civil defence services, from motives of real self-sacrifice. Everywhere there was a note of real heroism abroad. Many felt for the first time in their lives that they were really wanted for a worth-while cause. To hundreds of thousands it seemed that here was the first great adventure that life had brought them. In a word, life did seem in time of war a big and real thing, as contrasted with a state of little more than meaningless and futile existence, divided between dull drudgery in factory or office, on the one hand, and on the other the kind of relaxation, such as watching football or playing innumerable games of undistinguished golf, which had become habitual for hundreds of thousands in the days of so-called peace. It is obvious that those who attempt to crusade in the cause of peace must make it clear that what they desire is something very different from any kind of peace that the world has yet known. Perhaps then it is still true in this sense that war is not the worst of all evils. Perhaps the worst of all evils is the peace of selfish sloth, of acquiescence in remediable wrongs, of indifference to life's tragedy. But I do not think it is possible to deny that Dick's devastating denunciation of the evil of war is wholly just. War is not merely evil in itself; it increases enormously evil of all kinds. It is made an excuse for breaking in letter and in spirit every one of the Ten Commandments. It leaves behind it as an inevitable legacy a lowered moral standard in every nation, victorious or vanquished, which took part in it. And the chapter in *We Say "No"* called The Slayer of Souls is an indictment of the moral degradation war brings to so many of those who take part in it as true as it is terrible. I quote but one passage from that chapter, every word of which I can endorse from my own experience:

> "Some of us who were parsons were foolish enough to believe in the early months of the fighting [in 1914] that the ordeal through which the nation was passing would deepen and intensify spiritual values, and arouse

a new apprehension of the things of God. We learned as the years passed that men who live constantly in the shadow of sudden death are more apt to turn to the Devil than to God. They grasp frantically at whatever passing pleasure is offered, regardless of its price, because they know that tomorrow the fires of youth may be quenched for ever, and desire and dream be swallowed in the grave. I do not pretend to blame them. This corruption of youth is one of the inevitable consequences of war. It is part of the indictment that I bring against war as a slayer of souls" (p. 80).

Many who had no experience in the first world war have learned the truth of that indictment in the second. Is there a parish in the land which cannot furnish examples of the tragedy of homes broken through lust, to which the conditions of war inevitably gave rein? And it must be added here that the latest war did more even than its predecessor to undermine the moral standards not only of men but of women. "Your liquor is dear, but your women are cheap," was the dreadful verdict expressed by American troops who invaded the towns and villages of our country. It is not polite or tactful to say so: but truth has little regard for mere politeness, and unless we face it fearlessly, there is little hope of our learning the lessons of experience.

So Dick answered the question "Is war the worst of all evils?" in the affirmative—albeit with moments of doubt. But there are many sincere Christians who would agree with the great President Masaryk that "War is not the worst evil. To be a slave, to enslave others, is far worse." This was the view held, I think, by every archbishop and almost all the bishops in Dick's lifetime, and while the leaders of the Church sincerely held that view they were bound to disappoint Dick; but I think that where Dick was right was in his conviction that the Church's leaders were overbusy and preoccupied with the domestic concerns of the Church and gave too little time and thought to the great universal problems. And in all lands the Church's leaders laid themselves open to the charge that they put patriotism first and the Christian ideal second. Even the most flagrant warmongers among the nations could find church leaders ready to support their aggressions, and could carry out their wicked schemes assured that even if the church leaders did not openly support them few would dare to oppose them.

One of Dick's friends, Middleton Murry, wrote after his death, "No one looked to the Church for guidance in large-scale affairs. The Church would never have dared to give any. It knows its place. It knows its function: which is that of a good wife to the state. Like a good wife it never advises and never criticizes, and when there is a row it always stands up for its husband. And it insists on one thing as far as it may—that the husband shall keep out of the kitchen" (*The Betrayal of Christ by the Churches*, p. 15). Dick would have sadly agreed that there was only too much excuse for that bitter attack.

And Dick I think would have answered too Masaryk's plea that to be a slave or to enslave others is worse than war. "That may be true, but does war ever prevent enslavement or really free the enslaved?" What about the situation today? We have fought yet another war for freedom, but where is freedom to be found? It seems as though there were less freedom in the world than ever before, and most noticeably less in those countries we claim to have 'liberated.' War, it may be argued, merely sets people free from one oppressor to hand them over to another. Even in Great Britain today there is infinitely less freedom for the individual than there was before the war. We denounce Fascism because it enthroned the state and made the individual man its slave: but today the state arrogates more and more power to itself at the expense of the individual citizen, not only in Russia but even in our own country. How then can war be justified in freedom's sacred name?

§

Dick had to face in his own lifetime the charge which is always brought against all churchmen who plead publicly for church reform, that it is disloyal and shameful to "wash the Church's dirty linen in public." To which he might have replied that in the first place he did everything he could to get those in authority to perform that necessary operation in private; and in the second place that it was better that it should be done publicly, and by one who passionately loved the Church, than not done at all. There are far too many who are content to call attention to the official Church's glorious professions and refuse to acknowledge her weaknesses. And Dick felt that it was useless for the Church to summon the world to repentance unless she herself showed an example of true penitence. He remembered the tragic ineffectiveness of the National Mission of Repentance and Hope at the end of the first world war, when an unrepentant Church tried to convert the world, with singularly little result to show for a vast amount of propaganda. He did not believe that the Church could ever effectively lead the world into the paths of righteousness unless she publicly renounced the attitude of the Pharisee and adopted that of the Publican in her Lord's parable. The Church may always be excused for disregarding the attacks of those who hate her; indeed, for welcoming them. But she ought also to welcome the honest criticism of those who speak their minds only because they so love her that they long to see her set free from hampering traditions which, as in the Church of Israel in our Lord's own day, 'make the word of God of none effect.'

And, after all, though Dick himself never would have said so, he had seen at St Martin-in-the Fields what a church alive to the real needs of humanity could do, in a comparatively limited field; he was far too humble to believe that that was due to the fact that he was an exceptionally gifted individual, and he therefore was convinced that a church everywhere on fire with the Spirit, wholly consecrated to its primary task, could and would meet with an abundant response from those thousands of hungry sheep who seemed to him to look up and not be fed.

A question I have asked myself many times is this: What would Dick have done if he had lived to see the catastrophe he foresaw so clearly, and tried so hard to avert, fall upon the world?

I asked his (and my) great friend, Dr Maude Royden-Shaw, what she thought he would have done, when war broke out. She answered two things. First, she said that she could never discover that Dick had any policy in the event of war. He, with her and Dr Herbert Gray, had tried when the war between China and Japan first broke out in 1932, to get the League of Nations to sponsor a peace army of volunteers, who were prepared to go out and place themselves unarmed between the combatant armies, and die, if necessary, proclaiming the gospel of peace. Many will remember the letter signed by these three Christian leaders advocating this plan, which appeared in *The Times* and provoked a great deal of discussion at the time. This brave gesture came to nothing, but at all events it revealed the fact that there were many, not only in this nation but in many others, who were willing to give their lives in the cause of peace. But it was obvious that even if this venture could have been put into practice at the time it was suggested, it could never have been possible in the event of a world war. And Dick seemed to have no other policy or plan to put forward, though he would gladly have suffered imprisonment as a pacifist.

But during the same conversation Dr Royden-Shaw

told me that when she had discussed this very question with another of Dick's great friends, Canon J. M. C. Crum, who was one of his colleagues at Canterbury, the canon had said that he was sure that if Dick had lived to hear war declared, the shock of that declaration would have killed him. She agreed with this opinion. In reply to a letter of mine on this point Canon Crum wrote to me: "Let us accept it as a thing hundreds must have thought, that 1939 to 1946 would have broken a heart like his. I think—as reverently as it is in my power to think—of our Lord dying, *not* of the physical torture and exhaustion of the cross but of a broken heart, seeing our sin and seeing what *it* was in the sight of the Father—seeing *us* as an answer to the love of God! The physical surely was sacramental. The seen carried the unseen. So one may *talk*, but I don't see how Dick's eyes could see war as he saw it and it not kill his heart. We aren't meant to carry more or further than we can and his job was already, surely, as much as he could survive so long; and he was allowed to fall out, stand easy, dismiss and go into Peace."

That expresses, better than I could express it, exactly what I feel. Had he lived till 1939 Dick would assuredly have died of a broken heart.

But what if Dick had survived the second world war: if he had been with us today, in the flesh—that he is alive in that world which lies on the further side of 'the valley of the shadow of death' it is impossible to doubt—what would he be doing now? That he would have been saddened and depressed by the dreadful failure of men to learn, or even to attempt to learn, the lessons of the tragedy of our time goes without saying. That the victorious allies of the war are now divided by mutual suspicions and have apparently forgotten all the high promises and ideals proclaimed in the hour of danger would be indeed no surprise to him; for he would have pointed out while the war was still raging that unity based simply on common hatreds and common fears is the most precarious of all forms of unity: that the only unity which can last is that which is founded on love, which casts out fear. But I am certain that he would have been pleading, more passionately than ever, that it is hopeless for the churches to try to point out the way to unity to a distracted and divided world while they themselves are still hopelessly at variance. So he would have been urging, in season and out of season, all the churches to abandon all claims based on mere prestige and status, and inaugurate a united campaign in the cause of true peace.

I can imagine how he would have rejoiced with joy unspeakable over the great project of the Bishop of Coventry to build a centre of united Christian social service, intimately linked with the new cathedral that is to rise, a witness to life out of death, amid the ruin wrought by the war. No doubt he would have longed that the Roman Catholic Church should enter with all the others into this great scheme, but I can see him pointing out, with a chuckle of delight, that not only is the architect of the new cathedral a Roman Catholic, but also that the Bishop of Coventry, who was a friend of that great Roman Catholic artist, Eric Gill, has embodied the idea so strongly advocated by Gill of a central altar, in order that the corporate nature of the Eucharist may be emphasized.[1] And how he would have rejoiced in the Chapel of Unity, which is an integral part of the bishop's scheme. Here, at all events, he would have found evidence that the Church of England was making a great practical effort in the move towards closer unity among Christians for which he pleaded so often and so passionately.

Since this was written has come news which would have

[1] See *Eric Gill: Workman*, in this series; p. 26. Since this was written Sir Giles Gilbert Scott's plans for the new cathedral have been given up and it is not yet decided whether the altar in the new cathedral is to be central or not. The Chapel of Unity remains a part of the plan.

thrilled (perhaps *has* thrilled—who knows?) Dick's heart. On Sunday December 3rd 1946 the Archbishop of Canterbury himself made a suggestion "for discussion and examination," that the Anglican Church and the Free Churches should enter into full communion with one another, in the hope that that might lead in the future to a constitutional unity. How warmly Dick would have welcomed that suggestion. It is so exactly the kind of thing for which he pleaded so passionately: an archbishop of Canterbury giving just that lead from above for which he asked, for a forward move in the direction of the reunion of the churches, without which they can never hope to lead the world into the paths of unity and peace.

And in the wider world, how active he would have been in trying to get the politicians of all nations to see the essential foundation of any true and lasting peace. He would have tried, as he tried before the war came, to get permission to plead that cause in all nations, particularly, I think, in Russia; 'whether they would hear, or whether they would forbear.' He would have striven to awaken in the nations the feeling that the welfare of one was utterly bound up with the welfare of all. He would have backed up with all his might the efforts of the Bishop of Chichester and those working with him in the Save Europe Now campaign. He would have pleaded that if it is true, as one of the Prayer Book collects asserts, that "God . . . declares His almighty power most chiefly in showing mercy and pity," then those who profess to be followers of Jesus and to care for the preservation of a Christian civilization, must recognize and fearlessly proclaim that we should manifest our power, not by military might, but by showing mercy and pity to all those whom victory has placed in our power today. And he would have realized that at the moment—how agonizing this thought would have been to him!—the nations, for the lack of true Christian leadership, seem once more to be in grave danger of drifting towards the ultimate abyss, and he would, as always, have been prepared to give his life to help to save mankind from that awful fate.

Alas! there is no one now in the Church to take his place: no one who can stir men's consciences as he stirred them. "We see not our tokens, there is not one prophet more: no, not one is there among us that understandeth any more."

§

If we are to estimate rightly the significance of Dick's passionate pleas for a rebirth of the Church it is important that we should ask ourselves what we mean—and what he meant—when we think or speak of The Church. The very word "Church" has completely different connotations for different people, and indeed for the same person in one context or another. Thus when a man says "the Church has failed," in this or that way, he is invariably met by the indignant retort that he is blaspheming, since the Church is a divine institution, having Christ's own promise that "the gates of hell shall not prevail against it" and therefore cannot possibly "fail." Yet it does not require much thought to see that the two antagonists are using the word 'Church' in two completely different senses. The one is thinking of the Church in the sense in which St John the Divine used it in the epistles to the seven Churches of Asia. The other is thinking of the Church, in a mystical sense, as the Kingdom of God, the Body of Christ, the instrument of the Holy Ghost.

There are, in fact, two extreme types of believers, often radically opposed to one another. There are those who may be said to be primarily ecclesiastically-minded; and those who are essentially individualistic in their religious outlook. The former, valuing the Church on earth as a great historical institution, divinely founded, with definite orders, ordinances and rules (which are indeed necessary to its existence as a corporate body here on earth), are apt to treat the dictum "outside the Church there is no salvation" as though it applied literally to the Church on earth, which they think of as consisting solely of those who like themselves have been admitted to the Church by the traditional rites of Baptism and Confirmation. Those who are commonly called—and indeed pride themselves on being—strict churchmen hold firmly to this view of the Church.[1]

At the opposite extreme there are those who hold that salvation is purely a matter of individual faith in Jesus Christ as a personal saviour. For these the true Church on earth is simply the aggregate of those who have found personal salvation through faith in Christ. The Church on earth is an invisible unity. Its boundaries are known only to God, though any individual believer may know from his own personal assurance that he belongs to it.

The strict churchmen are for ever insisting on the duty of submission to the lawful authority and order of the visible Church. Those at the opposite extreme are for ever pointing out the gulf which seems to them to exist between the august claims made by the churchmen and the actual sinfulness of the visible Church as they see it. There is plainly little hope of any 'reunion' of those who hold these diametrically opposed views.

A Russian writer, formerly professor of philosophy in Moscow University, in a most interesting and valuable book[2] discusses these two opposed views of the Church and claims that each of them is partly right and partly wrong. He distinguishes between what he calls the "essential" or

---

[1] The dictum "outside the Church there is no salvation" is of course open to another interpretation, which is both true and of inestimable value: it is only not true if it is applied to the Church as a visible organization, with formal limits, here on earth.

[2] *God With Us: Three Meditations*, by S. L. Frank. Translated by Natalie Duddington, M.A. (Jonathan Cape).

"mystical" Church, on the one hand, and the "empirical" Church, on the other. The former embraces all men everywhere and throughout all history, before as well as after Christ, who have had a real experience of God and have lived by faith and have sought righteousness—all those Old Testament saints, for instance, who are enumerated in the eleventh chapter of the Epistle to the Hebrews and such pre-christian thinkers as Heracleitus, Socrates and Plato, who were regarded by the early Christian Fathers as "Christians before Christ." In this sense, he says, "the whole of mankind that has sought and anticipated Christ's truth throughout human history is included in His mystical Church" (*Op. cit.*, p. 249).

This Church is indeed super-temporal, necessarily Catholic, in the widest sense of that term, and necessarily one, because the Holy Spirit constitutes its essence and He "cannot break into mutually alienated and conflicting parts." The actual divisions of the Church on earth—the empirical Church—mean the parting of Christ's garment, but not "the tearing of His living mystical body to pieces." And Frank quotes another Russian as saying "confessional partitions do not reach to heaven." So too the mystical Church is necessarily holy, "because it is that *plane* of human life which is sanctified, illumined and permeated by holiness."

But the "empirical Church," although it is interpenetrated by the eternal, mystical Church, cannot be identified with it, as 'strict churchmen' often seem to take for granted. Being composed of sinful men it can never be perfectly holy. Being an organized society, and for that very reason obliged to have visible limits and for that reason to be exclusive, it can never be in fact truly catholic. And even if it can attain to a formal unity it can never be more than a unity which embraces divisions of opinion. The mystical Church is a divinely constituted organism: the empirical Church, though "the power upon which it rests and which helps it are supermundane and belong to the realm of grace," is after all "a reality of a purely earthly human order."

Dick Sheppard, whose vision of the Church was always of the mystical, essential Church, was distressed by the contrast between this ultimate reality and the empirical Church. He dreamed of a church here on earth which should manifest all the perfection of the mystical Church in its fulness. I do not believe that he ever thought out his theory of the Church. I do not think that he ever realized that while the world lasts the mystical and the empirical Church must always be in what Frank calls an *antinomic* balance, between two heterogeneous principles, because the very principle of the mystical Church is that of perfect freedom based on glad submission to one law only—the law of love; whereas the empirical Church must have a discipline and laws imposed and enforced under penalties by a human authority.

But while the perfect identification of the empirical Church with the mystical Church can never be accomplished, it is yet part of our duty as members of the empirical Church here on earth to strive without ceasing to make it a more and more perfect mirror and instrument of the mystical Church. Strong churchmen often make claims for the empirical Church which can only be rightly made for the mystical Church. The abolition of slavery, for instance, and the passing of the factory acts, are sometimes claimed as the work of the Church. It is quite true that these triumphs of the Christian spirit were carried through by men who were faithful members of the empirical Church and most certainly of the mystical Church; but in actual fact the empirical Church as an organization did nothing to bring these concrete triumphs about.

Dick was in truth a prophet of the mystical Church charged with a message of supreme importance to the empirical Church—what I have called elsewhere in this book the Official Church—to which even now the Church would do well to pay heed.

But it would be as wrong to think of Dick as holding the extreme individualistic view of the Church as a mere aggregate of individual believers, as to think of him as the kind of churchman who stands at the opposite extreme. He began his ministry as a loyal son of Cuddesdon Theological College, with distinctly "high-church" leanings. He had too great an affection for the Catholic tradition and the beauty of ordered and reverent worship ever to become a Protestant low-churchman. But the things which he counted of real importance were, first, personal love for and loyalty to Jesus Christ and secondly a church alive with the Spirit of Christ and therefore on fire with a passion to save the perishing world. The actual Church as he saw it did not seem to be on fire at all. He loved the story of Father Stanton, mounting the pulpit of St Alban's, Holborn, and crying "Fire! Fire!" and then adding (to the relief of the startled congregation), "everywhere but in the Church of England." He strove, in season and out of season, to prepare the way for a new awakening which he knew must come from the Holy Spirit. He knew that while it was natural and right that gatherings of clergy and laity should open with prayer for the Holy Spirit; it was equally important that the members of those gatherings should be prepared to welcome His coming, even if He came, as He so often does, in unexpected ways. Too often it is to be feared the prayer that is really prayed by pious folk would, if put into words, read, "Come, Holy Spirit—but come in the particular way we want, or not at all."

So, alas! the Holy Spirit comes and His coming is unrecognized, or even denied, by those who have not learned that "the wind bloweth where it listeth," and is bound by no human laws and confined in His operations to no human organization, however august it may be.

It is this that explains Dick Sheppard's impatience; it is the impatience of the prophet with the hardness of heart and blindness of eyes of those who are content with a merely conventional piety, a merely traditional churchmanship.

www.ingramcontent.com/pod-product-compliance
Lightning Source LLC
Chambersburg PA
CBHW070324100426
42743CB00011B/2546